Docker

The ultimate beginners guide to learn Docker step-by-step

Mark Reed

Table of Contents

Introduction

The age of virtualization has done a lot for allowing developers to build and create from their computers as if they were different systems. Virtual machines allow them to create entirely virtual operating systems within which to work and build. These systems are one of the major ways through which a homogenization process has been able to spread through the development world. A developer can run a Windows virtual machine from their Macbook in order to test the functionality of an app that was designed for Windows. It is far cheaper and easier to run a virtual machine than it is to buy a whole new computer.

Yet even virtual machines bring with them their own set of difficulties. There are many factors which determine how efficient a virtual machine will be on any given computer. Then, on top of that, each computer uses different hardware like graphics cards and processors. Two different Macbooks may each be able to run a Windows virtual machine but the underlying hardware has a direct effect on how well the app inside the virtual machine will run. So, while virtual machines have started a homogenization process, they are still far from completing it.

That's where Docker comes in. Docker is a platform as a service product which uses operating system level virtualization so that users can utilize software in packages which are called containers. Each container is isolated from each other and includes everything that the end user needs to run the software on their computer regardless of its specs. They're more lightweight than virtual systems and remove a lot of the guesswork from the virtualization process. Since Docker's creation in 2013, it has been used and expanded on by companies like Microsoft, Google, IBM, Huawei, Cisco and more. In fact, the use of Docker is spreading so quickly that an analysis of LinkedIn profiles in 2017 showed that mentions of the application went up almost 200% in 2016 alone.

So many people are finding that Docker is the perfect tool to solve their DevOps tasks that its continued adoption across industries and specializations shows no sign of slowing down. Chances are you found this book because you've already identified Docker as a potential tool for the problems that you face. The aim of this text is to give beginners everything they need to start using Docker themselves. To achieve this goal, this book is divided into two parts. The first part is the explanatory text which teaches you the concepts and steps that you need in order to use Docker. The second part is the exercises and hands-on training tasks which allow you to get started working in Docker to put what you've learned into motion. These exercises will be spread out throughout the book so that you can get right into them alongside the relevant sections.

The book is broken up into chapters which each focus on a specific element of Docker. Chapter One explores more of what Docker is and how and why it solves the problems mentioned above. We'll also learn what a Dockerfile, an image and a container is in this chapter.

Chapter Two will take you through setting up Docker on your own computer. There are some key differences in how Docker functions when it is run on Linux, Windows or Mac and we'll see what these differences are. You'll also run your first container in this chapter and see just how easy the process is.

Chapter Three will cover how we containerize an application. That is, how do we turn an application into an image which can be opened as a container so that we can share our apps with other Docker users. We'll take a look at how we deploy these applications and how we can share them with the wider Docker user base.

Chapter Four looks at networking with Docker. This covers how you can connect Docker containers together or even to non-Docker workloads in order to really make use of the full power of the Docker service.

By the end of the book, you'll be able to turn your applications into containers, share or run them through Docker and connect them to other containers and see just how powerful Docker really is. This is only a beginner's guide, so the more advanced topics aren't going to be covered here but everything you need to know to get started with Docker today is in your hands right now.

Chapter One:
Understanding Docker, Containers, Images and Dockerfiles

Docker can be a bit of a confusing program to understand if you've never worked with virtualization before. In order to clear up any confusion around Docker, let us take a look at what it is and why it exists. This will help you to decide if Docker is right for you or not. From there we'll look at the various components of Docker to understand what they are so that when we start using them in the following chapters there will be no confusion surrounding what each component does.

What is Docker?

Docker first launched back in 2013 after several years of development. At its core, Docker is a tool designed to make it easier to run applications throughout the DevOps process. Docker is like a virtual machine in that it runs on a computer but acts like it is its own computer. This allows for users to create, deploy and run applications through the use of containers, the main building block of Docker. Every piece of an application that is needed to run is included within a container, such as libraries and various dependencies, and this allows Docker to run those containers as if they were their own system. What's more, this allows for Docker containers to be shipped out to other users with everything they need to run the container included.

Docker is an open source platform, too. This means that anyone who wants to can contribute to Docker and use it to fit their own needs. If they find that Docker doesn't have a feature which they require, they can open up the program and add the features they want without having to worry about breaking any laws.

Docker enables users to separate their applications from the hardware and infrastructure they have in place to speed up delivery. Infrastructure can be managed in the same way that applications are. Together with the flexibility of the open source nature, this makes Docker a powerful tool in speeding up the shipping, testing and deployment of code to reduce time between creating it and testing it.

In action, what this looks like is as follows. The user uses Docker to download or open up an image file. This file is then deployed as a container. That container itself is a self-contained application. Instead of running a virtual machine in order to then run the application, the application itself is run like a virtual machine and the user can see if it works or not by whether or not it is working. This sounds redundant but it is an important note. If run in a virtual machine, the application not working may be tied to the virtual machine or the underlying hardware and so there are many reasons it may not work. In Docker, it doesn't work if there is an issue with the application itself.

With the What of Docker out of the way, let's turn now to the Why: Why is Docker gaining such attention in DevOps and the problems it solves.

What Problems Does Docker Solve (And When is Docker Not Recommended)?

There are several key benefits to using Docker in your DevOps workflow. These benefits make using Docker a great fit for many of your needs. Docker, however, isn't some magical program that will fit every need you may have. In looking at the benefits of Docker, it is important to also look at the times that Docker won't cut it. This way, you know for sure whether Docker is right for you. But first, let's look at those benefits.

One of the biggest benefits to using Docker is its isolation. Docker containers include all the settings and dependencies necessary to run them. This means that the dependencies of the container will not affect any of the configurations of the computer they are being deployed on. Nor will the containers mess with any other containers that may be running at the same time. When you run a separate container for each part of an application (such as a web server, front end and database that is used for hosting a web site), you are able to ensure that none of the dependencies conflict with each other. Containers could be designed to use entirely different underlying hardware from each other but run at the same time perfectly smooth through Docker's virtualization. This makes it much easier to ensure everything is running properly and makes sharing and deploying applications via container much simpler for everyone involved.

With this also comes a component of reproducibility. A Docker container is guaranteed to run the same on any system that is running Docker. The system specifications of a container are stored on what is called a Dockerfile. Sharing the Dockerfile with your fellow team members allows you to ensure that all images they build make use of that Dockerfile so that all the containers can run the same. This cuts out the guesswork of having to problem-solve issues relating to hardware.

The containerization of the various components of an application can offer a level of security. When an application is run in a traditional fashion, there is the risk that an issue with one component can cause the rest of the components to fail. When an application is run through Docker containers, a failure in one part can leave the other containers unaffected. This can make trouble solving much easier. Other security issues may arise, however, due to Docker's containerization. If security is important for your large applications, a more detailed look at your specific needs should be taken before using Docker.

Another benefit of Docker is the Docker Hub. Docker Hub is a directory of Docker images which have been put online and shared to be used by any Docker user who wishes to. There are many images and applications that can be found on Docker Hub. All you need to do to use them is download the pre-made images and put it into place. This can make your various Docker setups quick and easy. We'll see how to download and test Docker using Docker Hub in Chapter Two and we'll learn how to upload images to Docker Hub in Chapter Three.

Since Docker containers don't need to run an entire virtual operating system, it is much quicker and more effective to run Docker containers. A virtual system needs to run its own operating system and this can really tax the hardware being used. Since everything Docker needs to run is included in the container, the virtualized system takes hardly any additional resources at all. One of the great things about this is how much quicker it makes Docker when compared to a virtual system. What would take five minutes to boot on a virtual system takes closer to five seconds when used through Docker.

Because of all these benefits, Docker is particularly great for use in the following manners.

When you are learning a technology, you can use Docker in order to skip spending any time on installation and configuration. Since everything you need to run the program is included in the Docker container, you can launch the container to get your hands on new applications quickly to see if they interest you or are relevant to solving the various issues you are looking to tackle.

Docker is also fantastic for simple uses such as setting up and running a Minecraft server. Many simply applications such as this already have supported images available on Docker Hub and you can quickly grab them, deploy them and walk away. This can reduce the time necessary for setting up basic applications and get you up and running in a matter of seconds.

As mentioned above, isolation is a big feature of Docker and this is fantastic for running multiple applications on a server. You can reduce the amount of issues you have with a single server by keeping the various applications compartmentalized through Docker containers. This allows you to prevent any possible problems with dependency management that you may have to deal with otherwise. Teams can lose hours or even days trying to troubleshoot dependency issues which could have been avoided entirely through the implementation of Docker.

By far, the best use of Docker is for development teams. On any given developer team, there is sure to be a multitude of different setups in terms of hardware and underlying infrastructure. Since the use of a Dockerfile allows containers to be created with a uniform infrastructure in place, using Docker removes the variability between developer systems and allows for the exchange of applications and the testing of those applications to be streamlined. Cutting out the variability and decreasing the time between building and testing makes Docker absolutely amazing for DevOps.

At the same time that Docker makes DevOps smoother, there are, of course, areas in which it isn't the most effective tool to use. When it comes to the following situations, you are better off looking for alternatives to Docker.

If your application is too complicated, then a pre-made Dockerfile or a previously created image likely won't cut it. If you find that you are going to need to build, edit and handle communication between several containers spread across several servers then the amount of time necessary to get set up is going to be rather high and you will be better off looking for another solution outside of Docker.

You may also find Docker to be insufficient for your needs if performance is of critical importance for your application. Docker is far faster when compared to virtual machines but it still adds another cost onto the performance of the system it is running on. Running a process inside of a container won't be as quick as when you run that application on the system's native operating system. If every second matters for your application then Docker is only going to be a hindrance.

Docker is also still a new piece of technology and as such it is still under development. As new features are added to Docker, you will need to upgrade it in order to access them. Backwards compatibility between releases of Docker isn't guaranteed, though. This means that you may find yourself upgrading often and risking your entire setup every time that you do so. This level of uncertainty can be stressful to some, so consider it for yourself before adopting Docker.

Another downside is the way that Docker makes use of the native OS on the system it is running. We'll be looking at this in-depth in Chapter Two, but what it means here is that if your DevOps team is using multiple operating systems, then Docker won't fit your needs. In this particular case you are better off using virtual machines.

Because Docker was designed with applications that run on the command line in mind, Docker is not well suited for applications which require a graphical interface. There are ways in which you can run a graphical interface inside a Docker container, like making use of X11 forwarding, but even then these function poorly. If your application is of a visual nature, you are better using the native OS or a virtual machine.

Docker also has security issues which you should be aware of. Since the kernel of the OS is shared between the various containers in use, any vulnerability of that kernel is also present in your active containers. If you have a container that allows access to resources like memory then denial-of-service attacks could be used to starve the other containers active on the host system. Someone that breaks into a container could possibly break out of the container and carry over the privileges from that container to the host system. Docker images could also be poisoned and tampered with to make it easier for an attacker to gain access to your system if you aren't careful. This is especially bad if you use containers as databases for any type of secure information like usernames and passwords. All of these security issues are present and important to be aware of before you start using Docker.

As Docker continues to grow, many of these issues are sure to be addressed and fixed. The rate at which Docker is being adopted throughout the tech world almost guarantees that Docker is only going to become more secure and more comprehensive in the years to come.

What Are Containers?

A container is a unit of software that has been standardized. The standardization sees the software packaged along with all of the necessary code and dependencies required in order to run the application on any given computing environment. Containers have existed since long before Docker but Docker has popularized their use by simplifying the process of accessing and making use of them. Docker containers are lightweight and capable of standing alone. Everything that is needed to run the application is in the container except for the Docker program which can be downloaded freely and installed on any computer in a matter of minutes. Docker containers begin as images, which we'll look at in a moment. It is only once the image is run that it becomes a container itself.

A metaphor for containers that has been used often is that of a shipping container on a boat. Pretend you are shipping a bunch of office chairs. You could stack these chairs on the boat by themselves but they risk being thrown around by waves and other environmental factors. This is what is it like when you run applications on your native system and juggle conflicting dependencies and the like. The far easier way to ship those chairs would be to put them into a shipping container. Now the container is solid and locked in place so those chairs don't go anywhere when waves toss the ship around. If one shipping container falls off the ship, the others are still secure in their place. This is what using containers for applications is like: the containers secure everything within themselves to make it easier for the computer (the ship).

As mentioned previously, containers and virtual machines may seem quite similar to each other in that they both isolate resources and have similar allocation of said resources. Containers don't virtualize the hardware the same way that virtual machines do, though. A virtual machine is an abstraction of the physical hardware. You have your underlying infrastructure, then the virtual machine monitor on top of which sits the guest operating system in which your app will run. A container, on the other hand, is an abstraction at the layer of the app. You have your infrastructure, followed by the host operating system on which Docker runs and each container then runs through that. This allows for more applications to be handled by the system, quicker. It is important to note that Docker containers can be used together with a virtual machine if one so chooses and so, while they make for an apt comparison, they do not need to be thought of as replacements for each other in the strictest sense.

What Are Docker Images?

A Docker image is a kind of file which is used in order to run code in a Docker container. Made up of several layers, an image is built from the instructions for a working version of an application. When Docker runs an image file, it turns that image into a container. In the metaphor of the ship we discussed above, the Docker image would be the layout plan for how each shipping container would be laid out. Without the image, there can be no container because there would be nothing to make up the inside of that container. Another way to think of Docker images is to consider them to be a snapshot of the application in question. They are an "image" of the application running complete with everything it requires to run and so, when that image is then turned into a container, it has all of these elements present.

Each Docker image is made up to include the system libraries, tools and dependencies necessary for the executable code of the application it represents. Because an image is made up of multiple layers, developers are able to reuse image layers for different projects where applicable. The re-use of layers from images allows developers to save time since they don't need to make every layer of the image themselves. Images tend to start with a base image, though they can be made from scratch if necessary. The static layers of the image rest underneath a readable/writable top layer. Layers get added to the base image in order to finetune how the code will run in the container that opens. Each layer of the image can be viewed in Docker using simple commands (which we will be learning shortly).

When Docker opens a container using an image, a writable layer is created for the image. This new writable layer is called the container layer because its purpose is to host any of the changes that are made to the container while running. The container layer can store new files, modifications or deleted files. This allows the container to be customized rather than simple to run as a static application. Since these changes are saved as a unique layer on the particular instance of that container, this allows for multiple containers to run from the same underlying image but run uniquely due to what has happened on the container layer.

So, a Docker container is a running instance of a Docker image. Docker images are files made up of several layers in which all the information necessary to run a container is in place. If an image makes a container then the question that we still have left to answer is: What makes an image? For that, we need to talk about Dockerfiles.

What Are Dockerfiles?

Dockerfile is a text document which has all of the necessary commands that a user needs in order to assemble an image. A Dockerfile lets Docker automatically build images by following the commands in the file. Say you have grabbed a Docker image off of Docker Hub. When you launch that image, you will open up a corresponding container. But say you wanted to deploy multiple instances of that container from the single image you downloaded? Doing this can be a bit of a hassle. Or, say you downloaded an image for Ubuntu that was necessary for development but you wanted to modify the image to upgrade some of the software or add in extra packages that you require for your development project. In this case, you could go ahead and manually edit the image. If you have more than one image at hand that you need to work with, this again becomes a hassle. For all of these tasks, a Dockerfile could be used to quickly build the same image multiple times and save you from having to do it yourself.

Basically, the Dockerfile serves as the set of instructions that Docker uses to build an image. If we look at that shipping metaphor again, there is an important difference we can make between a cargo ship and Docker. Namely, it is a really big deal when you lose a container on a cargo ship. The metaphor also doesn't fit Dockerfiles very well. Another way of looking at it is to think of Docker containers like plants. When a plant dies, you can plant a new seed in order to replace it. The rest of the pot (the dirt and soil) remains the same and you will end up with a nearly identical plant. The plant is the Docker container, the sproutling is the image and this leaves the Dockerfile as the seed. By using the Dockerfile, you get the images which lead to the plants (Docker containers). While you could just use an image, using a Dockerfile provides you the advantage of ensuring that your build uses the latest versions available of the software in question.

To close out this chapter, let's look at the keywords that we will see used in a Dockerfile.

- ADD: This copies files from a source location on the host system and adds them into the container's filesystem at the destination that has been set out.

- ARG: Similar to ENV, this defines variables that users can then pass to the builder. ENV defined variables, however, will always override an ARG instruction of the same name.

- CMD: This is used in order to execute specified commands within the container in question.

22

- COPY: This copies files (or directories) from a specified location and then adds them to the filesystem of the image.

- ENTRYPOINT: This designates an application to be used every time a new container is created with the image.

- ENV: This is used to set environment variables which can be used to control how an application runs or to configure data locations. ENV variables can also be specified for later use within the Dockerfile itself. ENV set values will persist when a container is run from the image whereas ARG variables are only available during the build of the Docker image.

- EXPOSE: Is used in order to inform Docker that the container listens on the network port specified and is used to allow networking between the container and the world outside.

- FROM: This simply defines the base image that is being used to begin the build process.

- HEALTHCHECK: This tells Docker how to test a container to check if it is still functioning properly. When a container is checked and passes, it is healthy. If a container fails a certain number of checks in a row then it becomes unhealthy.

- LABEL: This adds metadata to an image.

- MAINTAINER: This defines a full name and an email address for the creator of the image.

- ONBUILD: This adds an instruction to the image to be executed at a later time when the image is used as the base of another build. Any build instruction can be set as a trigger.

- RUN: This is the primary way in which to execute commands.

- SHELL: This allows you to override the default shell that is used for shell commands.

- STOPSIGNAL: This is used to set the system call signal that is sent to the container in order to tell it to exit. By default, when you tell a container to stop, it is sent a signal then given a short period to exit gracefully before sending a stronger signal to kill the container. Using STOPSIGNAL allows you to override the default signal to set your own.

- USER: Sets the username that will run the container.

- VOLUME: Enables access from the container to a specified directory on the host.

- WORKDIR: Sets a path for where a command that has been defined using CMD will be executed.

There is a lot of information in here that isn't relevant to us while we are running simpler Dockerfiles. I have, however, included all of the possible Dockerfile commands in order to provide a reference which you can return to as needed. We will see these in action when we get to building Dockerfiles in a later chapter. For now, let us move to setting Docker up on our own computers.

Chapter Summary

- Launched in 2013, Docker is a tool that allows users to create and deploy applications in the form of self-container "containers."

- Docker is open source, which means anyone is allowed to tinker with it to add features that they desire.

- Docker allows users to separate the variables of hardware and infrastructure (to a degree) from the applications as containers include everything that an application requires to run.

- Containers run in isolation from each other and from the host system and this removes issues related to conflicting dependencies.

- A Docker container is also guaranteed to run the same on any system that is running Docker (so long as it shares the same OS kernel).

- Containerization components of an application can offer a level of security in which the failing of one part (or container) does not affect the operation of other active containers.

- Docker also makes use of Docker Hub, a directory of Docker images which can be downloaded to speed up the DevOps workflow.

- Docker containers are self contained and don't need to virtualize an entire operating system, which means that they run much faster and effectively when compared to virtual machines.

- Docker is especially useful for learning new technologies or setting up simple applications.

- The isolation of Docker containers make them fantastic for use on servers that need multiple applications running.

- The best use of Docker is for DevOps teams to cut out of the variables of infrastructure and shorten the time between building and testing applications.

- Docker is not a good fit when you have an overly complicated application or if you are looking to avoid regular updating to the newer versions.

- Docker is still a virtualized system which means that while it is quicker than a virtual machine, it is slower than running applications on the native OS.

- Docker makes use of the native OS to run, so a DevOps team would all have to be using the same operating system.

- It is important to note the security issues involved in using Docker and its graphical limitations.

- A container is a unit of software that has been standardized to run the same on any system. Containers have existed since before Docker but Docker has popularized their use.

- Everything needed to run an application is included in a Docker container, except for the Docker program which is available for free.

- A Docker image is a file made up of several layers which Docker runs in order to open a container.

- In order to run a Docker container, you must open it from a Docker image.

- A Docker image includes the system libraries, tools and dependencies that are necessary to run the application as a container.

- When a Docker container is opened from an image, a new writable layer is created for the image which is used to track any changes or customizations made to the application for that particular instance of the container.

- A Dockerfile is a text document that has all of the commands needed to assemble a Docker image.

- Using a Dockerfile can save the user a lot of time that would be spent opening multiple images, editing images or building images.

- There are 19 commands which may be used within a Dockerfile but Dockerfiles may be as simple as to only use 3.

- Using a Dockerfile to automate image generation rather than using a static image ensures that you get the most up-to-date version of the image in question.

In the next chapter you will learn how to set up Docker on your own computer. Docker functions differently depending on the host operating system and we'll see why this makes Linux the best operating system to use with Docker. You will also use Docker to open your first container to ensure that your installation is functioning properly. From there, you will learn about mounting volumes so your containers can get access to data on the host computer in real time. The chapter will then close out a lengthy and detailed exercise that walks you through the many common Docker commands that you will be using to control your containers.

Chapter Two:
Setting Up and Testing Docker

In order to start using Docker to containerize our applications and make use of the benefits discussed in the previous chapter, we first need to download and install it. In this chapter, you'll learn how to do this and run a "hello world" test in order to ensure it is functioning properly. Before we even get to downloading and installing, however, it is important to consider the operating system of the host machine you are planning to use Docker on. Whether you are using Linux or Windows/Mac is going to have a major impact on your experience of using Docker.

The Host Operating System – Docker on Linux vs. Windows/Mac

It is worth noting again that containers are not new inventions that came along with Docker. Containers were used previously to Docker in Linux. Docker simply introduced a local daemon process and a powerful REST API which made it easy to make use of the technology and sparked its widespread adoption. Docker also sparked Docker Hub which really took containers to the next level. The important thing to note about containers here is the fact that they are a part of the Linux ecosystem already. They are not, however, a part of Windows.

In terms of operating systems, Linux is designed far more effectively than Windows is. The kernel and file system that Linux uses far outperforms that of Windows. Because of this disparity in performance, containers were put into place to take advantage of the way that Linux is able to isolate processes. Docker was originally designed for Linux since container support was already present. It wasn't until late 2016 that Microsoft added support for Docker on native Windows 10 (the only other Windows system that Docker works with is Windows Server 2016). Before this announcement, the only way to use Docker on a Windows operating system was to use Docker Toolbox which was basically a virtual machine that ran an image of Linux. It was a good tool for learning how to use Docker but a horrible tool for actually putting Docker to use in any applications.

Despite all of this, there are some similarities in running Docker on Linux or on Windows. Docker containers will still function as self-contained applications. They can run natively without the use of a hypervisor or virtual machine. Containers can still be administered through Docker and they provide the same kind of portability on either system. Docker on Windows differs from Linux in that it is limited in the versions of Windows it can run on. Also, even though it can run on a particular version of Windows, it actually has far stricter requirements when it comes to the compatibility of Docker images. Networking features for containers are not fully supported on Windows yet, either. What is worse is that most of the systems used for container orchestration on Linux are not present on Windows and this reduces the functionality.

The biggest difference that makes Linux the best operating system for using Docker is the way that Docker makes use of the operating system. When you run Docker on Windows, you will need to run Windows-based applications only. Running Docker on Linux allows you to use the underlying Linux kernel to run applications that range across the various versions of Linux. When you run Docker on Mac or on Windows, they need to run Linux containers in a Linux virtual machine if they are to use them at all. This can lead to lots of slowdown that can cripple the host system if it isn't managed properly.

If you want to use Docker as efficiently as possible then Linux is truly the way to go.

Downloading and Installing Docker

While Docker is the most effective in Linux, you may have reason to want to use Docker in either Windows or Mac. Here you'll learn how to download and install it for whichever operating system you are using.

Downloading and Installing Docker on Windows 10

To use Docker on Windows you are going to need to download Docker Desktop. To do this, head over to the Docker Hub. If you have not set up an account yet then you can do this easily by following the "sign up" prompt and picking your Docker ID, putting in your email and picking a password. When you download the installer, you agree to Docker's Software End User License Agreement and their Data Processing Agreement, both of which are available to be read online.

Docker requires that you have Windows 10 64-bit. Pro or Enterprise work and so does Education so long as it is Build 15063 or later. You will also need to have Windows' Hyper-V and Containers features enabled. In order to run Hyper-V on Windows 10, your computer needs to have a 64-bit processor with Second Level Address Translation, 4GB of system ram and BIOS-level hardware virtualization support needs to be enabled in the BIOS settings.

The installer for Docker Desktop includes the Docker Engine, the Docker CLI client, Docker Compose, Docker Machine and Kitematic. In order to install just double click on the Docker Desktop Installer .exe file. An installation wizard will ask you to accept the licence, authorize the installer and then walk you through the steps of installation. You will need to authorize the Docker Desktop Installer by using your system password during the install process. You need privileged access to install the networking components, links to Docker apps and to manage the Hyper-V VMs. When approved, the installer will set everything up. Simply click "finish" when it prompts you and you can now begin using Docker Desktop on your Windows computer.

Downloading and Installing Docker on Mac

Head over to the Docker Hub to download Docker Desktop for Mac. Sign up if you don't have an account. By downloading Docker Desktop you agree to the terms of the Docker Software End User License Agreement and the Docker Data Processing Agreement, both of which can be read online.

In order to properly install Docker Desktop on a Mac you must be using a Mac that was created in 2010 or newer. These Macs have Intel's hardware support for memory management unit virtualization, Extended Page Tables and Unrestricted Mode. If you are unsure if your Mac has these then you can run "sysctl kern.hv_support" in the command terminal to check. If your Mac can support the Hypervisor framework then the command will return "kern.hv_support: 1". You also need to be using macOS 10.13 or newer. You will need at least 4GB of RAM and you must not have VirtualBox prior to version 4.3.30 installed, as any versions earlier are not compatible with Docker Desktop and can cause errors.

The installer for Docker Desktop on Mac includes the Docker Engine, Docker CLI client, Docker Compose, Docker Machine and Kitematic. After downloading the installer, double click on the .dmg file to open the installer. Drag the Docker.app file into your Applications folders. Once Docker.app is in your Applications folder then double click it to start Docker. You will be prompted to authorize Docker.app by inputting your system password upon first launching it. You will need privileged access to install the networking components of Docker. Opening Docker will create an icon on your top bar which lets you know that Docker Desktop is running and can be accessed from a terminal. When you first install the app, you will get a popup message that suggests the next steps you should take and will include links out to further documentation on using Docker.

Downloading and Installing Docker on Linux

In order to use Docker on Linux, you are going to need to have a 64-bit installation and a kernel that is at

3.10 or higher. Kernels that are older than 3.10 are unable to run Docker properly and are prone to data losses or kernel panics. Look for Docker on the Docker Hub.

You can run Docker on Ubuntu Xenial 16.04 LTS; Ubuntu Wily 15.10; Ubuntu Trusty 14.04 LTS; Ubuntu 12.04 LTS; Debian testing stretch; Debian 8.0 Jessie; and Debian 7.0 Wheezy. If you are using Debian 7.0 Wheezy then you are going to have to enable backports.

To enable the backports on Debian Wheezy, first log in and open up a terminal with "sudo" or "root" privileges. Then open "/etc/apt/sources.list.d/backports.list" with a text editor. If the file does not exist then create it. Remove any existing entries and add an entry for backports on Wheezy by writing "deb http://http.debian.net/debian wheezy-backports main". Then, update your packages with "apt-get update -y".

If you are using Ubuntu Precise 12.04 then you must use kernel version 3.13 rather than 3.10. You can upgrade your kernel by opening up a terminal and inputting "sudo apt-get update -y". Then install additional packages with "sudo apt-get install -y linux-image-generic-lts-trusty linux-headers-generic-lts-trusty". Use a graphical Ubuntu environment and run "sudo apt-get install -y xserver-xorg-lts-trusty libgll-mesa-glx-lts-trusty". Finally, reboot your system with "sudo reboot". This will ensure that you update your kernel and can run Docker.

You are also going to want to update Aptitude. Login with sudo privileges and open up the terminal. Purge older repositories with "sudo apt-get purge -y lxc-docker* && sudo apt-get -y purge docker.io*". After purging, you will want to update your packages with "sudo apt-get update -y && sudo apt-get install -y apt-transport-https ca-certificates". Following this you need to get the new GPG key with "sudo apt-key adv --keyserver hkp://p80.pool.sks-keyservers.net:80 --recv-keys 58118E89F3A912897C070ADBF76221572C52609D ". Open or create the file "/etc/apt/sources.list.d/docker.list" in a text editor and add an entry for your OS with the following list. Save the file after the entry is added and then update Aptitude again with "sudo apt-get update -y" and verify that it pulls from the proper repository with "sudo apt-cache policy docker-engine".

<u>Entries for OS</u>

Ubuntu Precise 12.04 LTS: deb https://apt.dockerproject.org/repo ubuntu-precise main

Ubuntu Trusty 14.04 LTS: deb https://apt.dockerproject.org/repo ubuntu-trusty main

Ubuntu Wily 15.10 LTS: deb https://apt.dockerproject.org/repo ubuntu-trusty main

Ubuntu Xenial 16.04 LTS: deb https://apt.dockerproject.org/repo ubuntu-xenial main

Debian Wheezy: deb https://apt.dockerproject.org/repo debian-wheezy main

Debian Jessie: deb https://apt.dockerproject.org/repo debian-jessie main

Debian Stretch/Sid: deb https://apt.dockerproject.org/repo debian-stretch main

With these steps out of the way you can then install Docker. First install the linux-image-extra kernel package with "sudo apt-get update -y && sudo apt-get install -y linux-image-extra-$(uname -r)". Then install Docker with "sudo apt-get install docker-engine -y".

Docker can then be opened using "sudo service docker start".

Exercise: Testing Your Docker Install

Now that you have installed Docker, it is a good idea to test it out and make sure that the installation went through properly. In order to do this, you will first check the version of Docker that is running on your system and then use it to run a simple "hello world" program.

Ensure you are using the latest version of Docker by running "$ docker version" in your command line. You will see Client, version, API version, Go version, Git commit, Built and OS/Arch information. Take note of the version that is displayed and double check it is the version you meant to install. To get the server version run "$ docker version --format '{{,Server.Version}}'".

If you had no problems checking your version then you have probably installed Docker properly but there is still room for some errors to have been made along the way. The best way to ensure that Docker is functioning properly is to run your first container. To do this, open up the command terminal again and run "$ docker run hello-world".

If everything works properly then you should see the following come up.

sh-4.2$ docker run hello-world

Unable to find image 'hello-world:latest' locally

latest: Pulling from library/hello-world

c04v14da8d14: Pull complete

Digest: sha256:0256e8a36e2070f7bf2d0b0763dbabdd677985 12411de4cdcf9431alfeb60fd9

Status: Downloaded newer image for hello-world:latest

Hello from Docker!

This message shows that your installation appears to be working correctly.

To generate this message, Docker took the following steps:

1. *The Docker client contacted the Docker daemon.*

2. *The Docker daemon pulled the "hello-world" image from the Docker Hub.*

3. *The Docker daemon created a new container from that image which runs the executable that produces the output you are currently reading.*

4. *The Docker daemon streamed that output to the Docker client, which sent it to your terminal.*

To try something more ambitious, you can run an Ubuntu container with:

$ docker run -it ubuntu bash

Share images, automate workflows, and more with a free Docker Hub account:

https://hub.docker.com

For more examples and ideas, visit:

https://docs.docker.com/engine/userguide/

If this is what you saw, then your installation is working perfectly. What is particularly great about using hello-world to test out Docker is the way that it walks you through exactly what it is doing. In the beginning, Docker first looks to where images are stored on the host machine, which is usually in /var/lib/docker/ when on Linux. Since Docker is unable to find the hello-world image at that location, Docker reaches out to the Docker Hub in order to download it. Docker Hub is where you downloaded Docker in the first place and it is also where all sorts of images are stored. You can run images that you don't have yet by doing the typical "$ docker run [image name]" input and allowing Docker to download the image. Docker pulled the image for hello-world from the Docker Hub, downloading the newest version available.

"Hello from Docker" begins the hello-world program proper and it walks you through exactly how it got it and what it did to run it. It even offers you an idea for something else to try, running "$ docker run -it ubuntu bash". Give that a try if you are feeling up to it, but for now we're going to continue looking at hello-world.

Since Docker had to go and download the image for hello-world when you ran it the first time, go ahead and run it again with "$ docker run hello-world". Notice how the first half of the message is

41

completely different? This is because Docker downloaded the image and is using the previously download image rather than reaching out to get a new one.

Congratulations on running your first Docker container. This means that your install of Docker is working properly and you are prepared to step into the world of containerized applications. Running hello-world is as easy as it gets, requiring just the simple "docker run" command. For this next exercise, we'll use our own hello-world application.

Exercise: Running a PHP hello-world in Docker

The outcome of this exercise will be another printing of "hello world" but getting there is going to be a much longer journey. To begin, create a new folder on your desktop specifically for this. This folder will just make it easier to keep everything in one place. Inside the new folder, create another folder and title this one as src (for source). Next, open up a text document. You're going to write a really simple PHP app. In the document, write:

<?php

echo "HELLO WORLD";

Save this file into your src folder and name it index.php. If you try to open this file, you'll see that it doesn't execute properly. This is because it requires a web server in order to work. But instead of downloading a web server and going through all that hassle, you're going to use Docker to take care of everything.

To do this, make a new file. Call this Dockerfile and save it in the first new folder you made. If you saved it properly then that folder should contain Dockerfile and the src folder. This Dockerfile will use code in order to create the environment necessary to run index.php. To do this you are going to need an operating system that has both PHP and Apache installed. Apache is the web server application that will be able to run index.php.

You saw in the last chapter that a Dockerfile is what tells Docker how to build an image and prepare everything. With this particular Dockerfile, we're going to use a pre-existing image from the Docker Hub to speed things up. We'll start with a pre-existing image and then build a little bit on top of it to get it working.

To find a pre-existing image, open up your web browser and head over to the Docker Hub. Log in so you can download and use the search functions and search for PHP. The Docker Hub has images from anyone involved in the Docker community that has taken the time to upload. When you are looking to work with images from Docker Hub, you need to look through the information to decide if an image suits your needs or not. The most trustworthy images on Docker Hub are labelled as official. PHP has an official release on the Docker Hub, so you can trust it to be well maintained.

When you click on the PHP image on Docker Hub you will be taken to a page that shows you all the variations of the image (called tags) and then information about the contents of the image beneath these. You want to grab the latest version of PHP, which you can see from the version number. Make sure you grab the latest version that also lists Apache, as you'll need the Apache web server application in order to run index.php. You'll notice how the tags are laid out in lines. As you go from left to right on a line, the information becomes more vague. It is best to select from one of the first two on a line, with the most information. The less specific the link, the latest version you get but it could also be unexpectedly upgraded and mess up your build. It is better to use the latest stable release rather than the absolute newest.

Scrolling down on the page reveals information about how to use the image. Most images have a section explaining what the software is and how to use the image on the command line. It even has information about how to create Dockerfiles using the image. For example, PHP shows you that you can use the PHP image in a Dockerfile by using:

FROM php:7.0-cli

COPY . /usr/src/myapp

WORKDIR /usr/src/myapp

CMD ["php", ",/your-script.php"]

This builds and then runs a Docker image which looks like:

$ docker build -t my-php.app .

$ docker run -it --rm --name my-running-app my-php-app

But since we're looking to run PHP with Apache, we need a slightly different Dockerfile. So scroll down a little more until you find the With Apache section. Here you'll see that to create a Dockerfile with PHP we'll need to use the following code:

FROM php:7.0-apache

COPY src/ /var/www/html

So what is happening here is that FROM is telling us the base image that is being used in the build. Then COPY creates a copy of the files in src/ and puts them in /var/www/html. Since the src folder exists on the host system, the container that opens from this image will not have access to those files. The container only has access to the files inside of itself. By copying src/

over to /var/www/html, the Docker container creates a version of the files it can access. Since this is a copy, anything we do to it in the Docker container doesn't affect the original file.

We named our folder src in order to match the code from the Docker Hub and make it easier. You can name the folder anything you want, however, so long as you note the name change when you are building the code. I invite you to go back after we finish building and play around with changing the name or the directory.

Since we're building our own Dockerfile for this, we want it to look a little different. Our Dockerfile should look as follows:

FROM ph:7.0-apche

COPY src/ /var/www/html

EXPOSE 80

To EXPOSE in a Dockerfile is to let Docker know that the container it is going to open will listen in to a specific port for networking purposes. If we created the Dockerfile but left out the EXPOSE, then the container would not listen to any incoming requests.

Looking back on the Docker Hub for a minute, if you don't know which operating system the image in question is using as its basis, click on the blue link to the right side of the image download. This opens up the code of the image and you can see a FROM which tells you which operating system is being used. The operating system listed here will have its own Dockerfile. These will stack up on each other and in this way you are able to layer images on top of each other to really speed up the process of building.

If you look at the PHP Dockerfile, you'll find it to be filled with a lot more information than ours has. It's a little more advanced than we're going to be getting into. But that's one of the great things about Docker: a lot of important releases are already up on the Docker Hub. Much of the heavy lifting with Docker has already been done. This actually makes it really beginner friendly. You can do a lot of things on Docker with very little complication, the difficulty scales with your ambition rather than overwhelms you.

So our Dockerfile is going to download PHP, copy our files and then listen at port 80 and then output a new image, the one we've just created. We'll be running that image in a moment. Let's build our file.

Open up a terminal. The first thing you need to do is move over to the folder that everything is in. You created a new folder on your desktop so use the change directory command to move there: "$ cd Desktop/Folder-name/. Then, you want to use "$ ls" to bring up the files available to use in this folder. You'll see your Dockerfile there.

To build it type in "$ docker build -t hello-world .". We're telling Docker to build the Dockerfile with the first command. "-t" tells Docker what name to give it; here we used hello-world. The next step is to tell Docker where the Dockerfile is located but since we're already in the folder we only need to put in a period. Run that.

If you've done this correctly then you should see that the Dockerfile needs to download all of the various layers that have been stacked on top of each other. First it will go and grab php:7.0-apache that it will need and this will continue until the layers have finished downloading. This is what is happening in our FROM command. After everything has been downloaded, the build then moves onto the COPY command and quickly moves everything over. It finishes up by running the EXPOSE so it can listen in at the specified port. At the bottom of these steps, you should see a line that reads "Successfully built XXXXX". This is the new image. Despite the fact that ours is called hello-world, the XXXX part of the name always just looks like a random mess of letters and numbers. Don't worry, the file will still be hello-world.

You have now created a Dockerfile and used it to create a container which you can use to run your earlier file. So open up the command line. You're going to now run your new image. Type "$ docker run -p 80:80 hello-world". You are telling Docker to run the specific file but we needed to add "-p 80:80" so that the host port is properly forwarded to the container's port. This allows requests to the host to be transferred over to the container so that the container can respond.

Run that and you'll see a whole lot of text pop up. Open up a browser and go to "localhost." If everything has worked then you should see a page that just reads "HELLO WORLD." The simple application that you made at the start of the exercise is now running in a container. PHP and Apache web server software are running in a container and your application is running on that software.

Try this challenge. Change it from "HELLO WORLD" to another message. If you can't figure out how, then the next exercise is for you.

Exercise: Updating Your PHP Application in Docker

Open up your index.php file again and change it from "HELLO WORLD" to another message. Anything you want. Refresh "localhost" to see your changes. Notice that there aren't any. Even though the original file has changed, the Docker container doesn't have access to the updated file.

When we built the image that is this container, the Dockerfile was told to COPY the contents of src. At the time of this copying, index.php only read "HELLO WORLD," not this new message. If we want to see this change then we are going to have to run that Dockerfile again to create a new image. Running that image will show the new message on localhost. If you are developing software then this can really slow things down. So now we must learn about volumes.

There are two kinds of volumes when dealing with Docker. The first kind of volume persists and is used to share data between containers. The second type of volume allows you to share files between the host and the container. Since we only have a single container that we are worried about, it makes sense for us to use this second kind of volume. Basically, you'll mount a folder inside the container as a volume. By doing this, you let the container see the files in that directory. Rather than just making a copy of the present files, this will allow the container to get access to the files in real time.

You want to work on the way this container works, so first click back over to your terminal and stop the container using "docker stop CONTAINER [name]". We're going to open the container again through the command line but this time we need a new piece added to our command. Our command originally looked like "$ docker run -p 80:80 hello-world". We are now going to add a mount command: "$ docker run -p 80:80 -v /home/[user-name]/Desktop/ Docker/src/:/var/www/html/ hello-world".

The "-v" command tells it that it is going to mount the src folder onto the folder in the container. It is important to note that you have to use the full directory path when mounting a folder, otherwise it won't work. Now run the file again by going over to the localhost. It should now read the updated message that you wrote. But this could just mean that it copied the updated index.php file from when you saved it last.

To ensure this is working properly, open up index.php and write something new. Save it. Refresh localhost. It's changed. Anything new you save in the PHP file is automatically reflected in the Docker container by hitting the refresh button. Docker isn't looking at a copy of the original file anymore, it has a live view of everything in the folder that you mounted. Keep in mind that you opened this image and built this container by looking at a directory on your computer. If you hand this Dockerfile off to someone else, they are going to need to adjust the directories and pathways on either their computer or on the file and command. If you are learning with a friend, trade

Dockerfiles and see if you can get them working on different computers.

The Components of Docker

Installing Docker doesn't just install a single application for use. Docker comes with the Docker Engine, Docker CLI Client, Docker Compose, Docker Machine and Kitematic. Each one of these components has its own role in the Docker system. A brief look at each of them will be useful in understanding exactly what you installed and what it is used for.

Docker Engine: Docker Engine is the foundational client-server technology that Docker uses in order to build and execute containers. When we have been referring to Docker throughout this book, it has been the Docker Engine which we are discussing. Docker Engine is made up of the Docker daemon, a REST API and a CLI that communicates with the daemon through the API.

Everything that is required to get containers running on your system is handled through Docker Engine. The Docker Engine creates a daemon process that allows containers, images, networks and storage volumes to all be hosted on it. It also manages the CLI.

Docker CLI Client: CLI stands for Command Line Interface and it is this client that allows the user to interact with the Docker Engine daemon through the Docker Engine API. All you need to do to build a container with Docker is to open up the command line and type "$ docker create [image-name]". This is possible because of this piece of the Docker software. Many of the Docker applications make use of both this CLI and the REST API.

Docker Compose: If you are using Docker extensively, then it can become pretty overwhelming to keep everything running smoothly. This is where Docker Compose comes in. Docker Compose lets you run multiple containers as a single service. If you have an application that takes two different components (say a database and a web server), you could launch them both as a service through the use of one file. Docker Compose uses YAML files which you can create using a vim editor.

Use "sudo vim docker-compose.yml" to create the Docker Compose file. You set out a "database" and "web" section in the file, these represent separate services to be run. The "image" keyword tells Docker what image to grab from Docker Hub. If you are using Docker Compose for the database/web server example above then you would also want to have a "port" tag in the database section so it knows which port to listen in on. Environmental variables required should also be set out here. An example using MySQL and NGINX would look as follows:

Services:

databases:

image: mysql

ports:

- "80:80"

environment:

- MYSQL_ROOT_PASSWORD=password

- MYSQL_USER=user

- MYSQL_PASSWORD=password

-MYSQL_DATABASE=demodb

web:

image: nginx

This would then be run through the command line with "sudo ./docker-compose up". Remember that this is assuming you name the file docker-compose.yml and that you are already in the same directory that you saved the file to.

With this command in place, Docker Compose will build the containers. All of the images necessary will download and the containers will launch when everything is in place. You can test and see if the containers have opened properly using the command "docker ps". We'll close out this chapter with a look at the most common and useful Docker commands.

Docker Machine: Docker Machine is another tool that comes when you install. There is a lot of confusion around the difference between Docker Engine and Docker Machine. What Docker Machine lets you do is run Docker Engine on virtual hosts and manage them through the command line.

Remembering that Docker was built for Linux and has issues when it comes to Windows or Mac. Docker Machine lets you run on those systems. You can also run Docker Machine on a data center, on a network or on a cloud provider. Before Docker v1.12 was released, Docker Machine was the only way available to use Docker on a Mac or Windows system.

Docker Machine is primarily used for one of two purposes. The first is if you want to access Docker on an older Mac or Windows system as discussed. The other reason to use Docker Machine is to provision Docker hosts on remote systems. If you have multiple Docker hosts connected (either locally, through a network or on the cloud) then you would use Docker Machine to manage them all from one system. Installing and using the command "docker-machine" allows you to create hosts, install Docker Engine on them and configure them. Each machine that is managed this way uses a combination of a configured client and a Docker host. In this way, you are able to use Docker Machine to control a series of Docker Engine setups.

Kitematic: Kitematic is used to make Docker easier to use on a Mac or a Windows system. Kitematic makes the Docker installation and setup process automatic. Kitematic also creates a graphical user interface for running Docker containers that is intuitive and easy to follow. Kitematic integrates with Docker Machine to install Docker Engine on your system. After installation, the Kitematic GUI loads up. The first thing it will do is show you an image that has been curated and which you could run immediately. There is also a search bar which you can use to find images from Docker Hub without having to leave the Kitematic GUI. The GUI has options for creating, running and managing all of your Docker containers just by clicking the corresponding button.

When you are using Docker on a Linux system, you use the CLI. Kitematic allows Windows and Mac users to have a graphical application with all the capability of the command line. Mac and Windows users, however, are not locked into using Kitematic. There is an option to switch between the Kitematic GUI and the Docker CLI; Kitematic, however, streamlines many of the parts of setup. For example, remember how you had to open up a port to listen to when working on the hello-world PHP exercise? When using Kitematic, it automates this aspect of running containers. It also automates the configuration of volumes.

If you have installed Docker on a Windows or Mac, then Kitematic makes it much easier to first dive in and start messing around with containers and images. We, however, will continue using the command line in our exercises.

Exercise: Learning the Basic Docker Commands

Since Docker was first designed without a GUI and relies so heavily on the CLI, it is a good idea to familiarize yourself with the various commands through which you control Docker. We'll close out this chapter by looking at these commands to see how they are used in action.

- Create a container from a Docker Hub image: Use *docker create* in order to create a new container. *$ docker create [image name]* reaches out to the Docker Hub to grab the image you named and create a new container from the image.

- List all Docker container: Once you start running multiple containers on Docker, you'll find yourself wanting to check and see if they are successfully created or if Docker ran into some issues with the container. To do this, run

$ docker ps. With this command, Docker lists out the containers that are running. When you run *$ docker ps*, the default option is to show you just those that are running. Add the *-a* tag (*$ docker ps -a*) to have Docker list all containers, including those that have been stopped.

- Starting a container: The container you created with *$ docker create [image name]* exists but it has not been run. To run it, use *$ docker start [container-id]*. Docker assigns an ID to containers when they are created. The *$ docker ps -a* command will show you the ID for your new container, use this with the start command to launch the container. You can check *$ docker ps* now to see if the container is running properly. If it had no issues launching then you should see it without the need to add -*a*.

- Connect to a container: Now that you have a running container, you will want to connect to it so that you can use it properly. Use *$ docker attach [container-id]* to do this. Now instead of operating on the host machine through your command line, you are now inside of the container. Anything that you do in the container will save in the writable container layer of the image.

- Stop a container: When you are done playing around inside of the container or it has finished its use, it is time to stop the container. To do this, you use *$ docker stop [container-id]*. This lets you stop a container. It is also an easy way to exit from a running container you are in. Note that since you are inside of your container in the current terminal (if you have been following along), you are going to need to open up a new terminal in order to issue the stop command. You need a terminal which is running from the host, the system that Docker is on, since you cannot control the host when inside a container. If you are inside a container then you can exit by typing "exit" or pressing control + D.

- Delete your container: Containers are self-contained, so if you have no more use for a container then you can delete it without causing any issues to your host system. This is one of Docker's big advantages. Type *$ docker rm [container-id]* and the container will be deleted immediately. Keep in mind that doing this also deletes any of the files or settings that you played with inside of that container. If you want to keep these but delete a container then you are going to need to back them up prior to deleting.

- Kill a running container: When you stop a container in Docker, what happens is the processes that are running inside the container are first stopped and then the container itself is closed down. When you use the kill command, Docker immediately shuts down the container as it is running on the host. Since the processes inside the container are just suddenly dropped, this can lead to problems with the container's processes or other issues. Stick with stopping your containers. If you are having trouble stopping a container and need to issue a kill order then use *$ docker kill [container-id]*.

- Detach from a container: You used the stop command to escape from a container earlier but doing this required you to shut down the container itself. There are plenty of times when you want to enter a container to run some commands and then exit, leaving the container to continue running. If you hold control and hit P, followed by Q (while still holding control), when you are inside a container then you can detach from that container without having to shut it down.

- Copy files from a container: There are many reasons you may want to copy the content of a container from the container to a filesystem. You may even want to copy files from the container to another container. This is done by using the copy command. Let's say you want to copy a specific file from the container onto the host, then you would run *$ docker cp [container-id]:/copy_file copy_file*. This will copy the file by the name of copy_file out of the container with that ID and put it on the host. If you want to copy files from one container to another container then you will use *$ docker cp copy_file [container-id]:/copy_file*. Using the index.php from your hello-world exercise, practice copying index.php from the container to the host. Launch an instance of the container that begins with making a copy of index.php and then hide the file and launch a new instance that doesn't have access to index.php. Use the *cp* command to move index.php from the first container and into the second one.

- Using commands in a container: When you attached yourself to your container earlier, you had to open a second command line in order to close down that container. The first command line was now inside the container and so it couldn't issue commands to the host. But if the command you wanted to use functioned inside of the container then you could issue them here; attaching to a new container anytime you wanted to issue commands inside it could eat up a lot of time. If you are running a complicated setup with a lot of containers then this is especially time consuming. Thankfully, it is possible to run commands inside a container from the host using *$ docker exec [container-id] [command]*. Using this, you are able to run commands inside a container without having to attach to it first.

- List all the images on host: As you've seen, images are how you build containers. When you grab an image from Docker Hub, there is a good chance that the image pulls its own images in the process. Use *$ docker images* to see all of the images available on your system. The images will come with information about their size, any tags they have attached to them and the repository that they can be found in. If all you care about is the image ID, then use *-q* to keep the data displayed at a minimum.

- Remove images: As your work with Docker progresses, you may find that you have images that you no longer use. These are just taking up space on your system, so why not remove them? Use *$ docker rmi [Image-ID]*. Note that if you have an image that is connected to more than one repository through tags then you need to use *$ docker rmi [repository]:[tag]*. If you are unsure whether an image is connected to more than one repository then use the image list command ahead of time to find out.

- Adding volumes to containers: We've already used volumes in order to update the localhost with the newest changes we made to our index.php file in the previous exercises. For that example what we did was link a folder on the host to a folder in the container so that the container could look at certain files on our host system in real time. We also saw that when we delete a container that we lose all of the data inside of it. If you want to be able to delete a container but keep the data then you will want to use volumes again but this time so that the data from the container can save onto the host. For this you will use *$ docker create -v $[directory path]:/var/www*. This will allow you to connect the directory to /var/www on the container.

- Use Docker Run: Following along with this exercise, the first thing you did was create a Docker container from an image and then started it using the *$ docker start [container-id]* command. You can shorten this process by using the Docker Run command to create and start the container. This is done with *$ docker run [image name]* command. Docker will first go and grab that container and then start it.

You'll notice that running this command will print out what is happening inside the command terminal. If you want to run the container in the background, without seeing the process in the terminal, then add *-d* before the image.

- Name a container: If you are working with several containers, you may want to name the containers for easier access. The name of a container can be used in place of the container ID (for many, but not all, Docker commands). To name a container during creation use *$ docker create --name [THE NAME] [image name]*. The container will take whatever is in place of [THE NAME].

- Expose a container's ports: We had to do this in order to properly use index.php. Containers are entire universes unto themselves, unless a port is exposed, so they can communicate with the host. Add *-p 80:80* to your create or run commands to open a port for the container to listen to.

- Examine the changes in a container: Debugging problems with Docker containers can be a time-consuming frustration. If something is misconfigured it can cause all sorts of problems, so it is a good idea to inspect the filesystem of your containers.

Don't just wait for a problem to arise: make a habit of checking from time to time to ensure smooth operation. Use *$ docker diff [container-id]* to go see what changes have been made in the container.

- Use a container to create an image: Remember that when a container is running, there is a new top layer added to the images. This is the container layer in which changes to the container are stored. This means that when you create and start a container, Docker automatically creates a new image by modifying a copy of an existing one. If you are working on an application that has multiple phases, you may want to create new images from a containerized instance of the application to reflect the changes you have made. By using the command *$ docker commit [container-id] [repository]:[tag]*, Docker will make a new image from the container.

- Check out Docker containers on a server: You can get real time information about containers, images and the like by using the command *$ docker events*. To see this in action, use that command in one shell and then create a new Docker container using another shell. Jump into that container and run a command or two. You'll see this information reflected in the terminal you ran *$ docker events* on. This is an especially great feature for when you're working with many containers or multiple people.

- View image history: Images can grow and evolve as you work through a project. Along the way, something may have gone wrong and you didn't catch it immediately. Checking out the history of an image can help you to figure out what exactly the image has been up to. First, use *$ docker images* to get the ID number for the image. Then use *$ docker history [image-id]* to get a report of how the image was created and other information, like size.

- View system wide Docker info: Filled with as much information as you could dream of, getting a system-wide view of Docker is as easy as using the command *$ docker info*. This will provide information about how Docker is interacting with the host machine, as well as how each of the running Docker containers are doing.

- Rename a container: We named a container above but we are only able to use that command when creating a container. If you already have a container in operation but want to give it a name then you need to use the rename command. This is done by using *$ docker rename [container-id] [the new name]*.

- Restart a container: When you have an issue with your computer, often the first thing that you are advised to do is to restart the system. This is the same when faced with a Docker container that is facing an issue. Use the command *$ docker restart [container-id/name]*. Note, you can use this command to restart more than one container at a time. Using this command will cause the container to restart in ten seconds. If you want to change how long Docker waits before restarting the container, add the flag *-t [integer]* after the command but before the container ID.

- Examine available networks: When it comes time to start networking with Docker and between containers, the first step is to see what networks are even available. To do this, use the command *$ docker network ls*. This will show you all of the networks that your containers can connect to.

- Connect to a network: Connecting a Docker container to a network is easier than you might think. Use the command *$ docker network connect [network name] [container-id or name]*.

- Disconnect from a network: When it is time to disconnect from a network then all you need to do is use the command *$ docker network disconnect [network name] [container-id or name]*. If you find that there is a problem with disconnecting from the network then adding the flag *-f* will force the disconnect.

- Create a network: Often used during the creation of an application, you may find that what you need is a personalized network that connects your containers together. Docker can make this for you with the command *$ docker network create [network name]*. There are many useful flags which can be added to this command to alter the parameters of the new network.

- View network information: Just like how you can get detailed, system wide information about Docker, you can get detailed information about the networks in use. Use the command *$ docker network inspect [network name]* to get information about the network in question. The *-f* flag can be added to have the readout formatted according to a favorite template or you can use the *-v* flag to make it a little easier to read.

- Delete a network: Now that you have made a network using *$ docker network create* *[network name]*, let's delete that network so it doesn't clog up the system. Use the command *$ docker network rm [network name]*. You can remove more than one network at a time by including multiple names.

- Delete all networks not in use: If you haven't been deleting networks as you stopped using them then there may be a whole lot of unused networks on your system. Use the command *$ docker network prune* to delete all of the networks that aren't being used. When you do this, you will be asked to confirm the removal of each and every network. If you want to avoid having to manually confirm all of this then the *-f* flag will automate the approval process for you.

- Remove unused resources: You may also have unused containers and volumes to go along with all of those unused networks. If you want to just remove everything that isn't in use then use the command *$ docker system prune*. Adding the *-a* flag will also delete unused containers and images from the runtime.

- Remove a volume: While a volume may have been necessary at one point in your production process, chances are you got past needing it at some point. When this happens, you can use the command *$ docker volume rm [volume* *name]* to remove the volume. Not that this deletes the volume that you have named. Use the *-f* flag to automate the confirmation process.

- Search Docker Hub: If you want to search for an image from Docker Hub, you don't need to open up the web browser. Use the command *$ docker search [image name]*. Docker will first look for the official image to match that name. You can add filters to your search to narrow it down.

- Delete a container on exit: Some containers only need to be used for a short period of time. You create the container, poke around in it for a moment and then exit and delete it. You can automate this process by setting the container to delete itself when it is exited. Use *$ docker run --rm [image name]*. Add bash or title as the container needs. The container will delete itself when you exit it.

- Grab networking logs: You may find yourself wanting the networking logs for your container networks for troubleshooting or other reasons. Get these logs on the host machine with the command *$ journalctl -u docker.service*.

- View help: You've just learn a whole lot of commands. Take your time going through them and trying them all out. You may already see some of the ways that these commands could be used together to create a really powerful setup for your DevOp needs. Docker provides a lot of documentation of its own that you can access through the command line. Use the command *$ docker* to get help with the Docker daemon. If you want to get more help on child commands then write out the command followed by *--help*. For example, if you want help with the network then use *$ docker network --help*.

Take your time practicing these commands. Many Docker users write out a cheatsheet with the most important commands listed on it as well as the most useful flags.

Chapter Summary

- Linux is a more effective OS than Windows and it had been using containers prior to the creation of Docker.

- Docker only works on Windows 10 and Windows Server 2016 but these have slowdown issues.

- Docker on Linux or Windows has many similarities. Windows, however, suffers from slowdown issues, poor networking implementation and container orchestration limitations.

- Docker on Linux allows for applications to run regards of the version of Linux they were designed for since they use the same underlying kernel.

- Docker on Windows or Mac only works effectively with native applications for those operating systems. To run Linux based containers on Windows or Mac you need to run a Linux virtual machine, which eats up more resources.

- To download Docker for Windows or Mac, head to the Docker Hub and download the respective Docker Desktop build.

- Docker Desktop has a GUI which allows you to control Docker through the click of a button rather than through a terminal or Powershell.

- Docker installs come with Docker Engine, Docker CLI client, Docker Compose, Docker Machine and Kitematic.

- If you're using Linux then you need to be running one of the following: Ubuntu Xenial 16.04 LTS; Ubuntu Wily 15.10; Ubuntu Trusty 14.04 LTS; Ubuntu 12.04 LTS; Debian testing stretch; Debian 8.0 Jessie and Debian 7.0 Wheezy.

- To use Docker on Debian Wheezy you must enable backports.

- Update Aptitude before installing Docker.

- Test your Docker install by first running the command *$ docker version*.

- Ensure that Docker is able to reach Docker Hub by running the command *$ docker run hello-world*. If you get back a message that starts with "Hello from Docker!" then your install is working properly.

- When you tell Docker to run an image, it first looks on the host system in the directory that is mounted. If it finds the image, it runs it. If it doesn't find the image then it reaches out to Docker Hub to see if they have the image in question. If Docker Hub has the image, Docker will download it.

- Running hello-world a second time will be different from the first because Docker no longer has to download the image.

- To run an application which requires a framework, such as index.php which requires PHP, you create a Dockerfile that grabs the necessary images.

- To run index.php, go to Dockerhub and find a version of PHP with Apache to use in the Dockerfile.

- When the Dockerfile creates the new image, it first pulls from the PHP image. That image in turn has information about the operating system it needs and so that gets pulled as well. Docker is very powerful in the way it can stack images in this manner.

- A Docker container needs to have a port exposed so that it can take requests from the host on that channel.

- When you copy index.php into the container, you can see index.php working. But to see changes to index.php you need to create a new image from the Dockerfile to open a new container because it only copied the file.

- In order to see changes to index.php in real time, you need to create a volume in the container. This is a folder on the host that is linked to the container so that the container pulls its file from that folder rather than just copying the files when the Dockerfile is launched.

- Docker Engine is the main technology that people are referring to when they say Docker.

It is what lets you build and execute containers.

- Docker CLI client is a command line interface that allows you to execute commands to control Docker.

- Docker Compose allows you to run multiple containers as a single service but is often only used by those who are well acquainted with Docker.

- Docker Machine allows you to run Docker Engine on a virtual host.

- Docker Machine is used to access Docker on older OS X or Windows systems or to provision Docker Hosts on remote systems that have been connected through a network.

- Kitematic makes Docker run better on OS X or Windows operating systems by providing a GUI to operate Docker through.

- Kitematic works for OS X and Windows but on Linux you will need to use the command line. You can use the command line or Powershell on OS X or Windows if you prefer it over Kitematic.

- You saw the many commands that Docker utilizes in the last exercise, this exercise also serves as a reference guide that you can return to as needed.

In the next chapter you will learn how to containerize an application by following the traditional Docker workflow of first creating and testing containers for each component of your application by creating Docker images. You will then learn how to assemble those containers into a complete application and test, share or deploy the complete application after it has been fully containerized. This will require the use of an orchestrator such as Kubernetes and management like Docker Swarm, which you'll learn how to install and setup. You'll also learn how to upload images to Docker Hub to share them with other users.

Chapter Three:
Containerizing Applications, Deploying them to Kubernetes and Swarm, and Sharing them on Docker Hub

Now that we have familiarized ourselves with Docker's commands and confirmed that our installation is working properly, we turn our attention towards containerizing an application of our own. We'll look at this process from two angles. The first exercise will use an example project from GitHub. The second will explore containerizing a legacy application. These two approaches will serve to give a detailed look at containerizing so that you can begin to containerize applications of your own.

Containerization will be followed by exercises to deploy our containers to Kubernetes and Swarm. Kubernetes and Swarm are two approaches to container orchestration which are used to help with scaling, networking and maintaining the applications you have containerized. In order to use both Kubernetes and Swarm, you will learn how to ensure they are installed and working properly on your system prior to deployment. Having learned all about container orchestration, we'll look at how you can share images on Docker Hub so that other people can benefit from what you have created.

Exercise: Containerizing an Example Project

The containerizing of applications through Docker has a developmental workflow which will become second nature the more often you work through this process. The first step is to create and test each and every individual container that is necessary to get all of the components of your application working. You do this through creating Docker images. After everything has been tested, the next step is to assemble the containers and whatever supporting infrastructure is necessary to form the application. This is expressed as either a Docker stack file or a Kubernetes YAML, which we'll look at in more detail when we get to deploying to Kubernetes. The third and final step is to test the containerized application, share it and deploy it.

To containerize an application we need to create the images that will produce our containers. Nothing happens in Docker without first having either an image or a Dockerfile which will build an image for us. Everything that our application requires will be captured in these images. Learning how to set up Docker containers for use as a development environment may take a little bit of work but once you have a grasp on this aspect of development, you will find that Docker makes it easier to set up a development environment than the more traditional approaches. Since Docker images have all the required dependencies inside them, there is no need to install anything else beyond Docker. We will, however, need to install the Git application for this example.

The first step you need to take is to download an example project from GitHub. If you don't have Git and are using Linux, then you should be able to install the Git tools by using the package management tool that comes with your distribution. On Fedora you can use the dnf: *$ sudo dnf install git-all*. If you are using a Debian distribution then use apt: *$ sudo apt install git-all*. You can install Git on a Mac by opening the command line and using the code *$ git --version*. For Windows based systems you will want to go to the website https://git-scm.com/download/win.

Git is a distributed version control system. Basically, what this is used for is to keep track of changes made to source code. It's a useful tool to help make collaboration more efficient and less prone to error. GitHub is a repository hosting service, similar to Docker Hub, that allows for code sharing. We're going to use Git to download a project from GitHub for use in this exercise. To do this, open up your command line and use: *git clone -b v1 https://github.com/docker-training/node-bulletin-board cd node-bulletin-board/bulletin-board-app*.

This will download what is a very simple application that functions as a bulletin board. The application is written in node.js. For the purposes of this exercise, pretend that you created this app yourself and are now interested in running it in a container through Docker.

Take a look at the files for the bulletin board application and you'll see that it comes with a Dockerfile. It should read:

FROM node:6.11.5

WORKDIR /usr/src/app

COPY package.json .

RUN npm install

COPY . .

CMD ["npm," "start"]

We explored how Dockerfiles worked already but let's just go over this one quickly. The FROM command tells the file to use the node:6.11.5 image as the first building block. This image in an official image and has been created by the node.js vendors and then validated by Docker to ensure that it is of the highest quality. This provides us with node.js which is what the bulletin board application was made in.

Next, WORKDIR points to /usr/src/app and lets Docker know that the actions that come after are to be handled in that directory. Keep in mind, this is telling

Docker about the image's file system and not the file system of the host system running Docker. COPY then makes a copy of package.json from the host and the period tells it that it will be copied into the present location, which we defined with WORKDIR. The RUN command executes npm install within the image's file system. To do this, package.json is read in order to ascertain the required node dependencies. These dependencies are then installed. COPY then grabs the rest of the application's code from the host and moves it over to the image. The CMD command is used to specify metadata in the image. This is used to describe how the container built from this image should be run. Here, it is telling us that this container is meant to support npm start.

So, from GitHub we got both a Dockerfile and the source code we need for the application. Let's build that image and test how it works. First step is to open up the command line and move to the directory node-bulletin-board/bulletin-board-app. From there, build the image using "*$ docker image build -t bulletinboard:1.0 .*". Docker will go through the steps outlined in the Dockerfile in order to create our image. You can tell this has been successful when your final message reads *Successfully tagged bulletinboard:1.0.*

Now, let's start a container from this image with *$ docker container run --publish 8000:8080 --detach --name bulletin bulletinboard:1.0.* Note the use of the flags here. --*publish* tells Docker that it is to forward incoming traffic from host port 8000 to the container's 8080 port. --*detach* is to tell Docker to run this container in the background. --*name* simply tells Docker to name this container, in this case it is named bulletin. We used the CMD command in the Dockerfile, so we don't have to tell Docker what process the container is to run. Docker will automatically run npm start inside the consider once it gets going.

To check if this worked, open up a web browser and head to localhost:8000. If it was successful then you will see the bulletin board application. This is a good time to run tests and ensure that the application is functioning as it was intended to. When you have confirmed it works properly then you can delete the container with *$ docker container rm --force bulletin*.

With this exercise, you took an application and containerized it through a few easy steps. In the next, we'll look at legacy applications. They're a little bit trickier.

Using Containers for Legacy Applications

In the tech world, a legacy app refers to an application which has grown outdated or obsolete. Despite this, there are many reasons that somebody might be interested in using the application. For example, you might have an old MS DOS game that you remembered fondly from when you were younger and want to revisit.

Legacy applications don't fall into a single set of defining features. There are several features, however, that are common among many legacy applications. They tend to use the local file system as persistent storage. In doing so, the data files and the application files are often mixed together. They run many services on a single server. Upgrading or installing them is a manual process that the user has to undergo and one that often has very little documentation to help guide them. Configurations are stored in files, once again mixed between data files and application files. Configurations are also often stored in more than one place. Legacy applications often use a process of communicating with the local file system rather than using TCP/IP. Most were designed under the assumption that there would be only one instance running and that would be on a single server.

There are quite a few disadvantages to the legacy approach, which is why it makes for an excellent exercise to really learn the ins and outs of Docker. For one, it is much harder to automate deployments of legacy applications. If you require more than one customized instance of the application, it can be quite difficult to use a single server between them and when a server goes down, it can be time consuming to get it back up and running since you have to do it manually. It's hard to roll back to an old version after deploying a new one and the deployment of a new one requires you to manually handle it. Because of all of these factors, you may find that your test and production environments seem to get away from each other which can result in unexpected errors when testing. It is also very difficult to scale horizontally through additional instances of the app.

For these reasons, containerizing a legacy application is far more difficult than the containerizing of the bulletin board application from the previous exercise. If you can wrap your head around legacy application containerizing then you will be able to handle just about any kind of containerizing.

There are some major benefits to containerizing legacy applications. Containerization makes deployment much easier and you can even automate deployments after containerization. A bad deployment can be rolled back by simply switching to a previous image rather than the laborious manual work it would take normally. Application updates also become much easier, whether they work or they fail. Since images make self-contained containers, switching between a production and test environment is flawless. A failed system is no longer a major hassle, since you can just launch a new container as a replacement. Since each instance of the application is in its own self-contained package, you can run multiple instances on the network and horizontal scaling becomes an option.

Basically, Docker containers offer solutions for pretty much every disadvantage that comes with using legacy applications. Let's see how we go about containerizing a legacy application and what considerations should be kept in mind throughout. For this exercise we won't be using a specific application like we did with the bulletin board application. Feel free to follow along with any legacy application of your choice.

Containerizing a Legacy Application

The first thing that we are going to do is make sure we know where persistent data is written in the file system. Every new application that we launch exists within a Docker container and this means that data stored in the container would be lost upon closing the container. Likewise, if the persistent data was kept inside a single Docker container then launching a new instance of the image would create a container that didn't have that information, it would still be in the previous container. So, persistent data must be written and stored outside of the container. While some legacy applications write data to a specific path, most of them store data all over the file system. Most even mix the data in with the application itself. Since we need to be able to keep persistent data, we have to figure out where the application records so that we can mount that location as a volume.

The next step of preparation is to identify which configuration files and values change depending on the environment. With Docker, our images are usable in multiple environments. Development uses the same image that testing uses, after all. Identifying which values change according to environment is important so that these can be configured at the start.

The final piece of preparation is to identify which services can be externalized. If the application uses services that run on the local machine, many of these can be easily externalized. Independent services or those that support communication by TCP/IP are perfect examples of these.

Now it is time to build the Dockerfile. Start with the operating system, then any necessary prerequisites and finally any scripts you have. This could look like:

FROM ubuntu:16.04

*RUN apt-get install -y [necessary packages] *

*&& apt-get clean *

&& rm -rf /var/lib/apt/lists/*

ADD . /app

RUN /app/setup.sh

WORKDIR /app

COMMAND /app/start.sh

Note that this example uses two scripts. Setup.sh is the app setup script while start.sh is the application startup script. If the application that you are looking to launch has all of its configuration as environmental variables then you don't need to worry about anything else. Environment dependent configuration values, however, will require an application startup script that can read the environment values and update the configured files. A startup script like this would look along the lines of:

set -e

cat >>/app/config.text <<END

my_app_config= "${MYAPPCONFIG}"

END

/app/bin/my-app --my-arg="${MYAPPARG}"

You will want to push the image after you build it. This means to put it onto a Docker registry so that it can be easily pulled onto the machine where it is to be deployed. If you are building this on the same computer that you are planning to run it then this step is pointless. We'll see how to push an image to a Docker registry later in the chapter. For now, let's look at deploying the application.

Deploying this container is a little more complicated than the previous ones have been. It would look as follows:

$ docker run -d -p 8080:80 --name [app name] -v /usr/local/var/docker/volumes/myappdata:/var/lib/mya ppdata -e MYAPPCONFIG=myvalue -e MYAPPARG=myarg --link db:db myappimage:mytag

We've already seen that the *-p* flag is used to let the container listen at a specific port. The *-v* flag tells it to mount the volume that is required for the persistent data we looked at above. The *-e* flag is used for the configuration of environment variables and you may actually need more or less depending on the application you are using. We use *--link* to connect the databases so that the application can communicate with them. The container will run in the background thanks to the detach flag, *-d*.

If you want to upgrade to a newer version of the application then you need to stop the old container and launch a new one from your new image. If you have to rollback to an older version of the application then you will also need to follow this. Keep in mind that rolling back or upgrading will result in downtime that should be factored into your decision to upgrade.

Running legacy applications through Docker may require a little more work setting up but Docker makes running legacy applications a thousand times easier than when those same applications are run off the host in the traditional fashion. There are, however, some considerations that you should keep in mind when working with legacy applications.

More often than not, legacy applications work by having multiple processes running at the same time. Because of this, you may find that orphaned processes build up over time. An "init" daemon would be used to clean these up naturally but Docker does not come with an "init" daemon. You can add a "init" daemon as an ENTRYPOINT when building your Dockerfile. A lightweight but efficient and well trusted "init" daemon is dumb-init.

While most Docker users have a tendency to run containers under the permissions of the root user, legacy applications have a tendency to have complicated user requirements. You may find yourself needing to run legacy applications under a different user or even under multiple users if you are running multiple instances. Because legacy applications require the mounting of volumes, this can be rather tricky since Docker's mount points are defaulted to root and any non-root processes won't have permission to write. This can be dealt with by creating directories on the host that are owned by the write UID/GID prior to launching the container. Another option is to adjust the ownership of the mount points on the level of the container when started.

Installing and Testing Kubernetes

Kubernetes is a container orchestrator that helps you to arrange your containers. It has tools for scaling, networking, securing and maintaining your containerized applications. The tools it offers are much more expansive than the options of the containers themselves, making it a powerful tool to use with Docker. This exercise was designed with Docker Desktop in mind, so if you are using OS X or Windows then you should check to ensure that Kubernetes is enabled.

If you are using OS X: After you have installed Docker Desktop you will notice there is now a Docker icon in the menu bar. Click on that icon and look for the preferences option. Inside the preferences, you will find Kubernetes listed. Check the box next to "Enable Kubernetes" and then save the setting by clicking on apply. Docker Desktop will now set up Kubernetes for you. Click on the Docker icon on the menu again and wait until the green light comes on beside "Kubernetes is Running." This tells you that it is running but you should still run a test to confirm that everything is functioning properly.

Open up a text file and write the following:

apiVersion: v1

kind: Pod

metadata:

name: demo

spec:

containers:

-   name: testpod

image: alpine:3.5

command: ["ping", "8.8.8.8"]

Now save this file as pod.yaml. What this file does is describe a pod that has a single container and that isolates a ping to 8.8.8.8.

Open up the terminal and navigate to the directory that you saved pod.yaml to. Check that the pod is up and running by using the command *kubectl get pods*. This should display back:

NAME: demo

READY: 1/1

STATUS: Running

RESTARTS: 0

AGE: Xs (where X is the seconds since creation)

Use the command *kubectl logs demo* to ensure that you get the proper logs for a ping process such as:

PING 8.8.8.8 (8.8.8.8): 56 data bytes

64 bytes from 8.8.8.8: seq=0 ttl=37 time=15.393 ms

Expect a few lines of this. The information here is only important in confirming that the ping process worked. You can delete the test pod now with the command *kubectl delete -f pod.yaml*.

If you are using Windows then you can follow the steps laid out above but in Powershell rather than a terminal; keep in mind that setting up Kubernetes with Docker Desktop on Windows may take upwards of half an hour between enabling and getting the green light to go ahead with the test.

Exercise: Deploying to Kubernetes

Did you notice that in commanding Kubernetes we used the word pod? This is because all containers in Kubernetes are scheduled as pods. Pods are groups of co-located containers which share some or all of the same resources. When dealing with applications and Kubernetes, it is very rare that you would ever create an individual pod. It is far more typical that you'll be scheduling deployments. Deployments are groups of pods which are scalable. Kubernetes maintains these deployments without the need for input. Objects in Kubernetes are described in what are called Kubernetes YAML files. A YAML file describes all of the components and configurations of the Kubernetes application. These YAML files are used so you can create or destroy your application with ease in any Kubernetes environment.

When you setup Kubernetes, you made a very simple YAML file called pods.yaml. In this exercise you will need a more complicated YAML file in order to run and manage the bulletin board application that you containerized earlier. Open up a new text document. This file will be called bb.yaml and it will look as follows:

apiVersion: apps/v1

kind: Deployment

metadata:

name: bulletin-demo

namespace: default

spec:

replicas: 1

selector:

matchLabels:

bb: web

template:

metadata:

labels:

bb: web

spec:

containers:

```
   -    name: bb-site
     image: bulletinboard:1.0

     ---

     apiVersion: v1
     kind: Service
     metadata:
     name: bb-entrypoint
     Namespace: default
     spec:
     type: NodePort
     selector:
     bb: web
     ports:
   -      port: 8080
     targetPort: 8080
     nodePort: 30001
```

Notice how this file has a line to separate it into two sections. This is because there are two objects in this YAML file. The first is a deployment and it describes a group of identical pods which can be scaled. It is set up to give a single replica of the pod. That pod is described under the template key. It has a single container. This is because we only need a single container to run our bulletin board application.

The other object being described in this YAML file is a NodePort service. This service will reroute traffic from the host's 30001 port to the pods's 8080 port so that the host system will be able to reach the bulletin board.

That this YAML file has two objects in it helps to illuminate an important aspect. It may be a lot of information there but both objects follow a pattern. It starts with the *apiVersion* key. This tells the program which Kubernetes API is required to analyze the object. This is then followed with the *kind* key, which tells us what sort of object is being described. This is then followed by the *metadata* key. *Metadata* is used to convey information about your objects such as giving them names. Then the objects finish with the *spec* key, which is used to apply all of the parameters and configurations the object needs.

With the YAML file built for the bulletin board application, the next step is to deploy it to Kubernetes. Open up a terminal and move over to the directory that you created bb.yaml in. Once you are in the proper directory, you can deploy the bulletin board application to Kubernetes with the command *kubectl apply -f bb.yaml*. This will give you an output that looks like:

deployment.apps/bb-demo created

service/bb-entrypoint created

This lets you know that the objects were made without any problems; you should still check that everything worked by having your deployments displayed. Check these by using the command *kubectl get deployments*. This will give you that feedback with columns for name, desire, current, up-to-date, available and age.

You should also check your services with the command *kubectl get services*. The services display will look almost identical to the deployments display but with information about the ports and IP addresses used by the services.

Pull your browser back up and head over to localhost:30001. If you see your bulletin board then you've successful deployed your application to Kubernetes. You can delete the application with the command *kubectl delete -f bb.yaml*. Next, we'll look at deploying with Swarm.

Installing and Testing Swarm

Like Kubernetes, Swarm offers tools for the scaling, networking, maintaining and securing of applications that have been containerized. Also like Kubernetes, these tools are far more powerful than those of the containers themselves. In order to deploy to Swarm, we will have to ensure that Swarm is properly enabled on Docker Desktop: this means using Windows or OS X as the host's operating system. Keep in mind that everything you need to run Swarm is built into Docker Engine and so Linux users can access it as well but without the GUI that comes with Docker Desktop.

For OS X users: Open up a terminal and use the command *docker swarm init* in order to initialize Docker Swarm. You will know this is successful if you receive a message that looks as follows:

Swarm initialized: current node (tjggogqpnpj2phbfbz8jd5oq) is now a manager.

To add a worker to this swarm, run the following command:

docker swarm join --token SWMTKN-1-3e0hh0jd5t4yj209f4g5qpowbsczfahv2dea9a1a y2l8787cf-2h4ly330d0j917ocvze30j5x9 192.168.65.3:277

To add a manager to this swarm, run 'docker swarm join-token manager' and follow the instructions.

You'll want to run a simple Docker service, such as one with an alpine-based file system, as a way of testing it out. Make sure to ping 8.8.8.8. To do this, you can use the following command:

*docker service create --name demo alpine:3.5
ping 8.8.8.8*

After creating the service, use the command *docker service ps demo* to ensure that it is running a single container. You'll get back information with columns for id, name, image, node, desired state, current state and error. You should notice that the error column is empty.

Next, double check that you can get the right logs when you execute a ping with *docker service logs demo*. If everything is fine then you should get some ping information like follows:

demo.1.463j2s3y4b5o@docker-desktop | ping 8.8.8.8 (8.8.8.8): 56 data bytes

demo.1.463j2s3y4b5o@docker-desktop | 64 bytes from 8.8.8.8: seq=0 ttl=37 time=15.32 ms

If everything worked correctly then you remove the service with *docker service rm demo*. Setup for Windows follows the same instructions with slightly different information fed back from the commands and with the use of a powershell rather than a terminal.

Exercise: Deploying to Swarm

First off, double check that Swarm is enabled by using the command *docker system info* and checking to see that it reads *Swarm: active*. If Swarm is not active then use the command *docker swarm init* to activate it. Double check *docker system info* to see that it now reads active. If *docker swarm init* does not activate Swarm, first try restarting your computer and testing it again. If this doesn't work then there is a problem with the install and you will need to go through the steps in the previous section again.

In the previous exercises in this chapter, you were able to create single containers to run the bulletin board application within. This is because the bulletin board application only has a single container. Swarm doesn't work this way, as it is incapable of building individual containers. This doesn't mean that it can't build an individual one, such as it will with this exercise, but that the container in question functions differently from what we consider to be an individual container. This is due to the automatic networking feature of Swarm. The workloads in Swarm are instead scheduled as services. Services are containers that have been grouped together in a scalable fashion. These grouped containers are combined with networking features that Swarm manages without need for user input. The files that describe and control objects in Swarm are called stack files. These are YAML files that have all the information about description and configuration that Swarm requires in order to create (or delete) an application within Swarm.

Let's use that bulletin board application again and build a stack file to help us manage it. Go ahead and open up a text editor and save this file as bb-stack.yaml. In the document, write the following:

version: "3.7"

services:

bb-app:

image: bulletinboard:1.0

ports:

-   "8000:8080"

So this file only needs a single object, which in this case is a service that describes a group of identical containers which are in turn scalable. With this particular build there will only be one container that is built using the image bulletinboard:1.0 (or whatever you chose to name the image when you first created it). You'll notice that we've also directed the container to listen on port 8000 and forward it to port 8080 within the container, a flag which should be quite familiar by this point.

Now this object is a service and we saw services in use when we used Kubernetes but it is important to note that services are not the same through Swarm as they are through Kubernetes. Swarm couples scheduling and networking features together to create new containers and route incoming requests their way.

Kubernetes, however, handles scheduling and networking as two different processes that have to be dealt with individually. With Kubernetes, deployments take care of scheduling containers as pods while services worry only about the networking of the pods.

Now that you have the stack file in place, it is time to deploy the application. You can use the command *docker stack deploy -c bb-stack.yaml demo*. You will know it has been successful if you receive the following message without any errors:

Creating network demo_default

Creating service demo_bb-app

Take a quick look at your stack file again. Notice how the only object you told it to make was a service. Yet when you ran the file, you got both a service and a network. This is an example of that difference between Swarm and Kubernetes we just discussed. A service in Swarm is a service and a network, the two are one and the same thing as far as Swarm is concerned.

As with everything, the first thing to do now is to check and make sure that the service is working properly. Use the command *docker service ls* to get all the services listed out. You'll get a report back with columns for ID, name, mode, replicas, image and ports. Pay attention to the replicas section. You'll know it is okay if it reads *1/1*. Keep in mind, this is because you were only looking to make one replica. 100% of the containers you told Swarm to make have been made. If it had read *0/1* or *1/2* then you would know that there was a problem in deploying the stack. Notice also that *docker service ls* here shows you how ports are being forwarded. If you open up your browser and head over to localhost:8000 then you should see the bulletin board application yet again.

Go ahead and close down the application with the command *docker stack rm demo*.

Swarm is a powerful tool that this exercise doesn't even begin to come close to fully utilizing. It does show you, though, how easy it is to use Swarm. If you were working with an application that requires multiple containers then you would write more than one object into the stack file. Swarm would then open these multiple containers, provided nothing went wrong, and network them together for you in the process. Swarm might be a simple tool but it is a great time saver and a powerful way to get your applications up, running and networked in a hurry.

Exercise: Sharing Images to Docker Hub For Others to Use

For this exercise, we will once again return to the containerized bulletin board application that we created at the beginning of this chapter. You used a Dockerfile to make the image that was run as the application's container. It is this image that you will share on Docker Hub. This way, you use the power of an online registry so that the image can be easily downloaded by whoever might need to use it. While our bulletin board application isn't particularly useful to other users, if you were to create a new application or an important piece of software, it is easy to see how pushing it to Docker Hub could be beneficial. Sharing an image on the Docker Hub is also highly attractive as it allows fellow developers on your projects to easily pull images that have been used in the project at hand.

Before you do anything else, you will need to set up a Docker Hub account. If you installed Docker yourself then chances are that you have already made an account to be able to download the installer. If you haven't yet, head over to https://hub.docker.com/ signup. Fill out what Docker ID you want, input your email and password and agree to the terms and conditions after reading them. You will need to check your email to confirm your account. After everything is confirmed, click on the Docker icon on your toolbar and click on sign in. Input your ID and password. If you prefer to use the command line then you can sign in using the command *docker login.* If there were no problems then you'll see your ID listed when you click on the Docker icon now.

With your account in place, it is time to push your first image to the Docker Hub repository. Begin by clicking on the menu bar Docker icon again. Look for the option that is labeled Repositories and then click on the Create option. This will take you to a page on Docker Hub that lets you create a repository.

Begin by filling out the name of the repository. In this case it would be bulletinboard or bulletin. You can change features such as making the image public or private but for now it is best to just leave the other options alone. Click the create button on the bottom of the page. You are almost ready to share your image but you have to first make sure that it has been properly namespaced. If you want to share an image onto Docker Hub then the image must be named in the following fashion:

<Docker Hub ID>/<Repository Name>:<tag>.

Open up the command line or Powershell and use the following command to rename the image:

Docker image tag bulletinboard:1.0 USERID/bulletinboard:1.0

You have to replace USERID with your unique user ID in order for this to work. Once you have properly renamed the file then you can push the image to Docker Hub by using the command *docker image push USERID/bulletinboard:1.0*. Now open the Docker Hub back up in your browser and you'll be able to see the new image that you uploaded is on the site. If you kept the repository as "public," like suggested, then this image can be found by anyone searching for it on Docker Hub or calling for it by name in their Dockerfiles or Docker commands.

It is important to note that what you have done here is to upload a Docker image onto Docker Hub. As you've seen throughout the book, there are many other files used by Docker such as Dockerfiles, YAML and stack files. Rather than pushing these files onto Docker Hub, it is better to make a habit out of storing these alongside your application's source code. One of the pieces that we left blank when creating our repository was the description section. A good practice is to use this description to provide notes or even links that tell users where they can find these other files. It can also be a good idea to use this description box to let users know how you made the image and how it is meant to work as an application. This way other users have all the knowledge and files necessary to make use of the image you pushed onto Docker Hub to the best of their ability.

Chapter Summary

- The first step in containerizing an application is to test each and every individual container that is necessary for running the application.

- You assemble the containers and the supporting infrastructure through Docker stack file for Swarm or a YAML file for Kubernetes.

- Git is a distributed version control system that we can use to grab a simple bulletin board application for use as a Docker training application.

- The Dockerfile for the bulletin board application tells Docker to start from node:6.11.5 and grab all the necessary pieces to run the node.js application we used in the exercises.

- The Dockerfile created an image of the bulletin board application and running this image with Docker gave us a containerized version of the application that worked so long as we allowed it to listen to the host through a port.

- A legacy application is an application that is outdated or obsolete. Running legacy applications on a host machine has many downsides that can make the process very frustrating. Using Docker to containerize a legacy application reduces those downsides vastly and makes the process far easier in the long run.

- Legacy applications need to to write persistent data and this requires us to find out where they save the data, which can be in several places rather than one centralized location. When we know where the data is saved, we can then mount these directories.

- The values and configuration of a legacy application may change depending on the environment; identify this to account for it in building.

- Many legacy apps were designed to only have a single instance on a server; containerizing the applications allow us to a way around this limitation.

- Running a legacy application through Docker takes a bit of work to set up but it can save you from hours of frustration trying to run a legacy app on host.

- Even when containerized, you should pay attention to make sure that your legacy applications aren't creating too many orphaned processes.

- The permissions required for some legacy applications may pose a challenge to be overcome.

- Kubernetes is a container orchestrator for use in arranging your containers. It allows you to network, secure, scale and maintain containerized applications with far more powerful tools than the containers themselves have.

- To ensure that Kubernetes is working, click on the Docker icon on the menu bar and look for the "Enable Kubernetes" button inside the preferences.

- Enabling Kubernetes on Windows may take up to twenty minutes. You will know it is ready to work when clicking on the Docker menu icon shows a green light next to the Kubernetes listing.

- Kubernetes containers are scheduled as pods. These are co-located containers which share some or all of the same resources as each other.

- Kubernetes is rarely used to create an individual pod. More often you use Kubernetes to schedule deployments, which are groups of scalable pods.

- Kubernetes uses YAML files which describe all of the components and configurations necessary to launch the pod or deployment.

- A YAML file will typically have at least two objects present: a deployment for the pods and a service. The deployment represents the pods and containers being made. The service is used for the purposes of networking.

- The objects in a YAML file are always described in the same order. First is the apiVision ket which lets Kubernetes know which API to use on the object. The Kind key describes the type of object. The metadata key conveys information like names. The spec key determines which parameters and configurations need to be made to the object.

- Deploying a YAML file with *kubectl apply [YAML file name]* will create the pod you have described. You will get a message if any errors were encountered but it is a smart idea to check *kubectl get deployments* and *kubectl get services* to see if everything has been built properly.

- Swarm is a tool similar to Kubernetes in that it allows for the scaling, networking, securing, and maintaining of containerized applications through the use of tools more powerful and efficient than those that containers have naturally.

- Swarm needs to be activated by checking *docker system info* and then using *docker swarm init* to turn it on if it hasn't been already.

- Swarm is not used for creating single containers but rather Swarm schedules services which are containers that have been grouped together to be scalable. These containers are combined together through networking features that Swarm manages automatically.

- Swarm uses stack files, which are YAML files that have been written for use with Swarm rather than Kubernetes.

- A stack file only needs to describe a single item, which is called a service.

- A service in Swarm is different from a service in Kubernetes. Kubernetes uses one object to schedule and another to network. Swarm only needs to describe a single object, a service, which focuses on the scheduling of the containers. This is because Swarm naturally networks the containers together for the user.

- Deploy a stack file with *docker stack deploy [stack file name]*. Again, it will tell if there are any errors but you should check *docker service is* to make sure everything is working properly.

- When checking *docker service ls* after using Swarm, pay attention to the column labeled replicas. You should see a number like 1/1 or 4/4. This means everything was deployed properly. If the equation isn't full, such as 1/4 or 2/5, then there has been an issue in deployment.

- Swarm's networking power makes deploying multiple containers and networking them together as easy as writing a stack file for your application's needs.

- Docker Hub is a powerful tool for Docker users since it serves as a repository for hundreds of thousands of Docker images. You can push your own images onto Docker Hub to allow others access to them as well. This is useful for sharing with the wider world or even just among members of your development team.

- In order to push images onto Docker Hub you need to make a Docker Hub account to receive a Docker ID. Use *docker login* or click on the login button on the Docker icon from your menu bar to login after signing up.

- Click the Docker icon, select Repositories and then Create. This takes you to a page to create a new repository.

- You will have to name the repository here. You can also add a description of the image or set it to only be shown privately. Setting an image to private allows you to create a backup of the image online without letting other people find it.

- An image has to be properly named to be allowed on Docker Hub. The name has to be in the fashion of *<Docker Hub ID>/<Repository Name>:<tag>*. You can rename a file by using *docker image tag [file name] [USER ID]/[repository name]*. Use your user ID and the name you assigned the new repository.

- Docker Hub is used to share images but Dockerfiles, YAML and stack files are important pieces of using Docker. Store these elsewhere but link to or describe them in the new repository's description box so that others can find or create what they need to use your image.

In the next chapter you will learn all about the ins and outs of networking with Docker. There are several kinds of networks which Docker uses. These are bridge, overlay, host and macvlan networks. Each of these networks has its own purpose and rules for operation. You'll learn about each of these and follow along with exercises to set up and explore your own networks. You'll also learn how to disable networking in a container and the way that containers perceive their networks.

Chapter Four:
An Introduction to Networking With Docker

The containerization of Docker is a powerful tool in and of itself but the hard truth of the fact is that if all Docker did was create containers then it wouldn't be gaining the popularity that it has been. That popularity comes from Docker's ability to network containers together. We briefly touched on some of the networking features that Docker uses when we tackled the exercises in the previous chapters. We've really only just scratched the surface of Docker networking.

In this chapter we will first take an overview of networking in Docker to get a sense of what is and isn't possible. From there we'll move into using bridge networks, overlay networks, host networking and macvlan networks. There will be exercises along the way, of course, and we'll also take a look at how we can disable networking for specific containers. With this in place, you'll have all the knowledge you need to get started with Docker in your DevOps workflow today!

An Overview of Networking in Docker

As we've discussed previously, Docker can be used on Linux, Windows or Mac OS X. Rather than go into those elements related only to a specific operating system (such as iptables on Linux or Windows's routing rules), our discussion on networking in Docker will focus on the broader actions that can be performed with Docker. There will still be plenty of exercises which you will be able to learn from. Let us start by looking at the network drivers which make up the core of Docker's networking power.

First up is the bridge. This is the default network driver which you will use the most often. If you don't select a specific driver when you are creating a network then Docker will select bridge automatically. A bridge network is most often used to connect containers to each other so that they can communicate and work with each other. These networks are best used when the containers that you want to communicate are all running on the same host system.

Host is used to remove the network isolation which is in place by default. When you create a container with Docker, that container is kept separately from the host system. If, however, you want your container to be able to directly access the host's network then you use the host driver. The most appropriate use of a host network is to allow a container access to the host's network stack while still keeping the container isolated in its other functions.

An overlay network is used to connect several Docker daemons to each other. It is also used to allow Swarm services to reach each other. An overlay network can allow a Swarm service to communicate with a stand-alone container. It can also allow two stand-alone containers to communicate even when they are on different daemons. Overlay is most appropriate when you have containers running on different host systems but still need them to talk, or when several applications are required to work together despite being on different swarms. The overlay setup allows you to remove routing at the level of the operating system.

The macvlan network is used to give a container a MAC address so that your network reads it as a physical device. The daemon will route any traffic to the container through the assigned MAC address. The macvlan driver is often used in the beginning of using Docker where you may be migrating from a virtual machine to a Docker setup. It is also one of the better choices for networking legacy applications which function by communicating with a physical network rather than a network stack.

One driver that you can use is the none driver. As the name suggests, you select none in order to disable networking in the container. Often this is done in order to allow a user to then run a custom network driver; however, custom drivers are well beyond the scope of this volume. If you are interested in custom drivers or seeing what other plugins are out there, you can find many third-party drivers on the Docker Hub or across the internet. Just understand that using a third-party driver comes with its own security risks. Always do your homework on plugins before using them.

We'll be turning our attention to bridge networks in a moment but it is worth first mentioning that Docker Enterprise (Docker EE) has two networking features which the free version of Docker does not. Docker EE comes with HTTP routing mesh, which allows users to share network IP addresses and ports among more than service. Docker EE also features session stickiness, which allows you to put information in the HTTP header for UCP (Universal Control Plane) then uses it to route requests to the specified service task. These features are not included in the version of Docker that we have been discussing in this book and so we will not be using them in the following exercises.

Docker Bridge Networks

When it comes to networking, a bridge network is a device on the Link Layer which is used to forward traffic from one network segment to the next. It can be a piece of hardware or software, so long as it is running on the host machine's kernel. Docker's bridge networks are software which allow containers to communicate with each other so long as they are on the same bridge. If you have containers running that are not on the bridge then they will not be able to communicate with those that are. Containers running on different bridge networks can not communicate with each other but can communicate with those containers sharing their specific bridge. In this manner you can have several bridge networks activated at a time. Bridge networks don't work for containers running on different Docker daemon hosts; for those you will need an overlay network.

A default bridge network is created when you start Docker. Containers you create automatically connect to the bridge network unless you specify that they should not. You can, however, create a user-defined bridge network which is far more powerful than the default.

A user-defined bridge network is able to offer your containerized applications more control over the isolation and interoperability. When you connect a container to a user-defined bridge network, it automatically exposes all of its ports to the other containers on that bridge while obscuring ports from anything outside of the network. User-defined bridges also provide automatic DNS resolution to the containers on the network while containers of a default bridge network need to use IP addresses to access each other. To remove a container from a default bridge network, that container needs to be stopped and then recreated if you want to move it to another network. Containers can easily be connected or disconnected from a user-defined bridge without needing to first stop it. User-defined bridges allow for more configuration options. Finally, it is worth noting that containers on a default bridge network all share the same environment variables. This is something that is almost impossible to achieve with a user-defined network. If you need containers to share environmental variables then the default network is better but otherwise it is wiser to use a user-defined bridge network.

Exercise: Using a Default Bridge Network

For this exercise, first grab an Alpine image off of Docker Hub. We will be using the Alpine image to create Alpine containers which we will then network through a bridge.

After you have grabbed the images, open up a terminal and use *$ docker network ls* to list out the networks that are currently running. If you haven't created a network yourself or a swarm then you should see three different networks listed here. You should see a bridge, host and none network and see

118

that they are using the bridge, host and null drivers, respectively. The host and none network are not fully functioning networks in and of themselves but rather are used to connect a container to the host or cut off a container from contacting any network. For our purposes at the moment, we will only be focusing on the bridge network.

Use *$ docker run -dit --name alpine1 alpine ash* and *$ docker run -dit --name alpine2 alpine ash* in order to launch two instances of Alpine as a container. The *-dit* flag is used to launch the containers in the background with interactivity and a TTY while *ash* is used to launch Alpine in its proper shell. Notice that you did not specify a particular network with the *--network* tag. Because they were not told a specific network to connect two, both of these containers are now running on the bridge network. Check that the containers have opened up without a problem by using *$ docker container ls* and confirming their status.

Next, you will want to inspect the network. Since we are using the bridge network, we check it by inputting the command *$ docker network inspect bridge*. This will return a whole lot of information. You will notice a *bridge* tag near the top. This is where information about the network itself is found. As you look down the information that was returned, you will find a *container* tag which tells you about the containers connected to the bridge network. Take note that the *bridge* section includes the IP address of the gateway between the Docker host and the network and that the *containers* section includes the IP addresses for each of the containers active on the network.

Since you opened up the containers in the background, you will have to use *$ docker attach alpine1* to connect to the first container. You'll notice that the prompt becomes # because you are the root user. Once in, use *# ip addr show*. This will let you see the way that the container is interfaced with the network. This should return two pieces of information for you. The first is a loopback device and the second is a broadcast which will have an IP address listed. If you compare this IP address to the one you saw a moment ago when you inspected the bridge network then you will see that it is the same.

Sticking inside the container, you should use the ping feature to confirm that you are able to connect to the internet. Use *# ping -c 2 google.com*. The *-c 2* is used to limit the ping to only two attempts. You should see a reply that looks similar to this:

PING google.com (172.217.3.174): 56 data bytes

64 bytes from 172.217.3.174: seq=0 ttl=41 time=9.841 ms

64 bytes from 172.217.3.174 seq=1 ttl=41 time=9.897

-- google.com ping statistics --

2 packets transmitted, 2 packets received, 0% packet loss

Round-trip min/avg/max = 9.841/9.869/9.897 ms

This tells you that your ping was able to reach its intended target, google.com. Next, try pinging your second container by using *# ping -c 2 [IP ADDRESS]*. The IP address of the second container can be found above where you used the *$ docker network inspect bridge* command. The ping message that is brought up should look almost identical to the previous one but you'll notice that the time it takes is much shorter. Try pinging the container again by using its name and you will see that it fails. It needs to be done with the IP address.

Exercise: Using a User-Defined Bridge Network

If you completed the above exercise on default bridge networks then you should already have an Alpine image to work with. If you have not yet downloaded an Alpine image then go to Docker Hub and acquire one now. For this exercise, we are again going to work with two containers running Alpine but instead of connecting to the default network we will instead create our own network. We will be using two more Alpine containers, one that is connected to default and another which is connected to both the default and our new one. Let's start by creating the new network.

Use the command $ *docker network create --driver bridge alpine-network*. This tells Docker to create a new bridge network called alpine-network. Notice that we use the *--driver bridge* command here. Technically we don't need to. Since bridge is Docker's default style of network, we could have just used the command $ *docker network create alpine-network*. But it is useful to see the *--driver* command in action as this is the command we'll be using to create other network types later.

Next, use $ *docker network ls* to list out the networks. You'll see that now you have alpine-network as an additional bridge network. You should see two bridge networks, a host and null. Let's take a deeper look at our new network by using $ *docker network inspect alpine-network*. You'll find the IP address for the network. Open up a second terminal and inspect your default network with $ *docker network inspect bridge*. Notice that the gateway IP addresses are different from each other. You should also see less information when you look at alpine-network here compared to what you saw on the default network in the previous exercise. This is because we have yet to run and connect any containers to it. Let's create those containers.

We're going to create all four containers here with the following:

$ docker run -dit --name alpine1 --network alpine-network alpine ash

$ docker run -dit --name alpine2 --network alpine-network alpine ash

$ docker run -dit --name alpine3 alpine ash

$ docker run -dit --name alpine4 --network alpine-network alpine ash

Remember at the start that we plan to connect one of these containers to both the alpine-network and the default bridge network. We haven't done this yet. Why? This is because we are going to need to use another command if we want to connect to more than one network. When using *docker run*, you can only connect to a single network at the time. To connect the fourth container to the default network, use *$ docker network connect bridge alpine4*. Then make sure that all of the containers are running properly with *$ docker container ls*.

Now, let's check out networks. Start with the *$ docker network inspect bridge* command and you will see that alpine3 and alpine4 show up (including their IP addresses, copy them down now). Using *$ docker network inspect alpine-network* will reveal alpine1, alpine2 and alpine4 all connected.

Remember how we needed to use the IP address to ping a container on the default network in the last exercise? Let's try that again but using one of the containers attached to the alpine-network. Start by attaching to one of the containers with *$ docker container attach alpine1*. Now let's start pinging. Begin with *# ping -c 2 alpine2* and you will see the expected ping results showing how long it took. Try this with *# ping -c 2 alpine4* and *# ping -c 2 alpine1*. Each of these returns the same successful information. Now try *# ping -c 2 alpine3*. It returns *ping: bad address 'alpine3'*. This is because alpine3 is not on the alpine-network. Try using the *# ping -c 2 [alpine3's IP address]* command. Now the result shows that the address is accepted but the ping fails, 100% packet loss. Detach from alpine1 by holding down CTRL and pressing P then Q.

Now, you connected alpine4 to both the newly created alpine-network and the default bridge network. Since it is connected to both networks, it should have no problem pinging the other containers. Let's connect to it with *$ docker container attach apine4*. Once attached, start testing your pings beginning with *# ping -c 2 alpine1* and moving through to alpine 2, alpine3 and alpine4. You should see that all of the pings worked except for alpine3, which has once again come back to us with *ping: bad address 'alpine3'*. So, try the command *# ping -c 2 [alpine3's IP address]*. Surprise, it pinged properly!

This is because alpine4 is connected to both of the networks and so it can access everything on either one.

If everything has worked as it was supposed to so far then chances are that there are no problems in either of the networks. Nevertheless, it is always best to double check them by pinging google. We are already attached to alpine4 so let's begin with *# ping -c 2 google.com*. Detach from the container and use *$ docker container attach alpine3* in which you will then use *# ping -c 2 google.com* again. Repeat this step for each of the four containers that are running Alpine. They should all come back with successful pings.

Congratulations, you have successfully created and run a user-defined bridge network. Finish up by closing down the network. First, stop the containers with *$ docker container stop alpine1 alpine2 alpine3 alpine4*. Then, remove the containers from Docker with *$ docker container rm alpine1 alpine2 alpine3 alpine4*. Finally, remove the user-defined bridge network with *$ docker network rm alpine-network*.

Docker Host Network

While Docker's bridge networks are isolated networks for containers to attach to, using the host network is a way for containers to be less isolated.

Typically, Docker containers are used specifically for their isolation but there are times when you may not want this to be the case. Using the host network will allow for a container which functions using the host's IP address. In previous chapters we created containers which forwarded to port 8080. If we create a Docker container which binds to port 8080, we would be able to communicate with that container through port 8080 through the host's IP address. Using the host network also removes options related to port-mapping, as this requires a container to have its own IP address.

Using the host network can help to improve the performance of the containers and it is an especially useful tool for use with containers that use many ports. Using the host network removes the need for network address translation, since rather than mapping an IP address, all the system needs to do is use one already in place. It should be noted, though, that only the Linux version of Docker supports the use of host networking and so if you are using Docker on a OS X or Windows system then this option will be unavailable to you.

You can use the host network in conjunction with a swarm service but the traffic necessary to manage the swarm will be sent via an overlay network. If you choose to use the host network with swarm then the individual containers of the swarm will have access to the host network while the control traffic makes use of the overlay. Doing this creates its own limitations that can cause a headache trying to sort out.

Exercise: Using the Host Network for a Docker Container

This exercise is only viable for those that are on Linux systems. If you are using Windows or OS X then you can skip to the next section. Either use Docker commands or head to the Docker Hub and download an NGINX image for use in this exercise. We will be running NGINX directly through the host network. Doing this will actually create a container that is both isolated and not. This may sound paradoxical but it isn't. What happens when we use the host network is that the NGINX application will function as if it were running directly on the host, except that the files, storage and namespaces will function in isolation from the host. Essentially, it will be as if the NGINX container has one foot in isolation and one foot on the host.

Begin by launching the container. You will want to do this as a detached process, so this means using the *-d* command. We will also setup this container so that it removes itself when it is exited, which we do with the *--rm* command. In order to achieve this, our command will need to look as follows: *docker run -- rm -d -network host --name test_nginx nginx.*

Now, when you head to http://localhost:80/, you will reach NGINX. NGINX automatically bonds to port 80, so if the host was already using port 80 then you won't be able to access NGINX this way. If port 80 on the host is busy then you will need to use the *-p 8080:80* flag while creating the container. Note that you don't need to use 8080 itself but rather the port of your choosing so long as it follows this template.

Use the *ip addr show* command in order to take a look at your network interfaces. Unlike the previous exercises, we're looking to see that a new process was not created. Look to see which process is bonded to port 80 with *sudo netstat* command. Since you are using the host network and not one of the Docker networks you need to use the *sudo* command because it is the host system which owns the process.

When you are done, you can use the command *docker container stop test_nginx* to stop the container. The container will then remove itself automatically because you created it with the *--rm* flag in place.

Docker Overlay Networks

Using the driver for an overlay network creates a distributed network that is active between more than one Docker host. An overlay network sits above host-specific networks, such as bridge networks, in order to allow for secure communication between connected containers. Using an overlay network, Docker takes care of routing packets first to the proper host and then to the specific container required.

If you create a new swarm or join an already existing swarm then you will see two new networks through that Docker host. The first is an overlay network which is named ingress. This overlay network is used to take care of data and controls related to the swarm services. A swarm service that is created with a user-defined overlay network automatically connects to ingress. The second network that is created is the docker_gwbridge network which is used to connect Docker daemons to each other.

You can create a user-defined overlay network with *$ docker network create -d overlay new-overlay*. This type of overlay network can be used for swarm services. By adding the *--attachable* flag to get the command *$ docker network create -d overlay --attachable new-attachable-overlay* you create an overlay network which stand-alone containers can also connect to. This simple flag creates an overlay network with a much different functionality than the default overlay.

Let's explore how we make use of each. Take note: in order to use the overlay networks of the following exercises, you will have to have at least a single-node swarm. If you have been following along with the exercises then you will have run *docker swarm init* previously. If you haven't, then go back and look at the exercises on Docker Swarms before you continue.

Exercise: Using Docker's Default Overlay Network and Creating a User-Defined One

If you have been following along then you will already have an image for Alpine. If not, head to Docker Hub and download one now. This exercise will also require that you have three physical or virtual hosts to run Docker. These hosts should all be connected to the same network without a firewall. Throughout the following exercise the hosts will be called manager, worker1 and worker2. The two workers will only be able to run service tasks but the manager can run service tasks and manage the swarm at the same time. You can set up Ubuntu hosts on a cloud like Amazon EC2 if you don't have enough hosts already.

The first thing that we have to do to explore the default overlay network is to create our swarm and have our three hosts join it. Using the manager host, start the swarm with *$ docker swarm init --advertise-addr=[manager's IP address]*. In the text that is printed, look for the token and write it down. The token is required to allow the worker hosts to join the swarm. Note that the *--advertise-addr* flag is only necessary if the host has more than one network interface.

Switch over to worker1 and join the swarm. Afterwards, you will do the same on worker2 but switch any reference to worker1 to reference worker2 instead. That command looks as follows:

*$ docker swarm join --token [TOKEN] *

*--advertise-addr [Worker1's IP address] *

[Manager's IP address]:2377

Switch back over to manager and use *$ docker node ls* to see all available nodes. You should see three nodes return, which represent manager, worker1 and worker2. If you use *$ docker node ls --filter role=manage*r then you should only see the manager. Using *$ docker node ls --filter role=worker* will return worker1 and worker2.

If you use *$ docker network ls* on all three, you will see that each host has an overlay network called ingress now. You should also see a bridge network under the name of docker_gwbridge. Docker_gwbridge is used to connect the ingress network to the host's network. This allows traffic to flow to the swarm managers and workers and then back again. Any swarm service created without a specific network joins ingress. When you are creating groups of applications it is a good idea to use different overlay networks for each application. Let's create two default overlay networks to see how this is done.

Create a new overlay network using the manager with *$ docker network create -d overlay nginx-network*. When either worker1 or worker2 begin to run a service task which is using this new network they will be connected to it automatically, so you don't need to worry about creating anything on them. Keeping on manager, create a NGINX service on nginx-network with five replicas:

*$ docker service create *

*--name nginx-service *

*--publish target=8-, published=80 *

*--replicas=5 *

*--network nginx-network *

nginx

Next, run *$ docker service ls*. This will allow you to see the progress of the service. Since we're launching five, it may take slightly longer than normal. When everything is up, inspect nginx-network on all three hosts with *$ docker network inspect ngnx-network*. You will notice that worker1 and worker2 both see nginx-network despite the fact that you never created it on them. Docker did this for you automatically. In the output that returns from the inspection, you should notice that it is much longer than any inspection you've run previously. The containers and the peers sections should be especially lengthy since there are three nodes and five services. Heading back onto the manager, use *$ docker service inspect nginx-service*. Keep track of the information on ports and endpoints.

So our first network is in place but we want to use two networks so let's use the manager to create another with *$ docker network create -d overlay nginx-network2*. With this second network created we can then update our services over to it. This is done as follows:

*$ docker service update *

*--network-add nginx-network2 *

*--network-rm nginx-network *

nginx-service

Run *$ docker service ls* and you will see that the services have been updated. You should also notice that they have been redeployed. Using *$ docker network inspect nginx-network* will show you that the containers that had been connected to it are longer present. Using the command *$ docker network inspect nginx-network2* will show that the containers are active there now.

You have now created a second default network and moved your services over to it. This is what you should do when you need to run multiple applications or application groups which are expected to work together.

Exercise: Creating a macvlan network

Macvlan networks are especially useful when dealing with legacy applications or those which are used to monitor the traffic on a network. This is because these applications are designed with the expectation that they will be connected to a physical network. Note, there are other applications that expect this as well beyond just the two types mentioned above. When you are working with an application of this sort then using a macvlan network is needed. The macvlan driver is used to assign each container a MAC address. This tricks the application into thinking that it has been connected to a physical network interface which is itself connected to a physical network. Basically, it tricks the containers. In order to do this you need to have a physical interface designated on your Docker host for the macvlan network to use. It will also be used for the subnet and gateway of the macvlan network.

It is important to understand that it is easy to accidentally damage your network using a macvlan because of IP address exhaustion or VLAN spread. This happens when you have a large number of MAC addresses attached to your network. You will also need networking equipment which can handle what is called promiscuous mode, which is used to allow a single physical interface to have multiple MAC addresses. Because of this, if the application you are working with is capable of using a bridge or overlay network then it is almost always better to use one of those as this will lead to less issues during long term use.

A macvlan network can be created in one of two modes: bridge or 802.1q trunk bridge mode. Bridge mode allows traffic to move through a physical device located on the host. In contrast, 802.1q trunk bridge mode moves traffic from an 802.1q subinterface that Docker creates as required. 802.1q trunk bridge mode is used to give you control over the routing and filtering of traffic at a much more detailed level.

Let's start by creating a bridge mode macvlan network to route traffic through a physical network interface. When doing this we need to use the *parent* tag in order to tell Docker which interface the traffic will be going through. In this example we will use *eth0 pub_net*. If, for some reason, you want to exclude a specific IP address from being a part of the macvlan network then you will add the command *--aux-address="name=IP address to be excluded"* before the parent. Creating the network will look as follows:

*$ docker network create -d macvlan *

*--subnet=IP address of subnet/24 *

*--gateway=IP address of gateway *

-o parent=eth0 pub_net

Creating an 802.1q trunk bridge mode macvlan network is very similar. The key difference here is that we use a dot in the parent category to tell Docker that there is a subinterface to the parent. Docker will read this and create the subinterface for us. So this code looks as follows:

*$ docker network create -d macvlan *

*--subnet=IP address of subnet/24 *

*--gateway=IP address of gateway *

-o parent=eth0.50 macvlan50

Exercise: Networking With a Macvlan Network

With an understanding of what a macvlan network is used for, in this exercise you will attach a container to both a bridged and an 802.1q trunk bridge macvlan network. Before starting the exercise, there are a few notes which should be considered. You will most likely need to have physical access to the networking equipment you are using because most cloud providers block macvlan networking. Also, like the host networking driver, the macvlan driver only functions on Linux and only on a Linux kernel that is version 3.9 or higher. Finally, we will be using eth0 as our ethernet interface but you should check the name of your device and use that in place of eth0.

If you have not yet grabbed an Alpine image then do so now on Docker Hub.

Let's begin with a bridged mode macvlan network. Here, traffic will flow through eth0, after which Docker will notice it and then use the assigned MAC address to send it to a container. Start by creating a new macvlan network by using:

*$ docker network create -d macvlan *
*--subnet=IP address of subnet/24 *
*--gateway=IP address of gateway *
*-o parent=eth0 *
test-macvlan-network

Using *$ docker network ls* should reveal the new network and using *$ docker network inspect test-macvlan-network* will confirm that it is working properly. If so, then the next step is to start the Alpine container. Attaching a container to a macvlan looks quite different from the normal commands for creating a container. You'll be using the following:

*$ docker run --rm -dit *
*--network test-macvlan-network *
*--name macvlan-alpine-exercise *
*alpine: latest *
ash

137

You already know that the *--rm* flag signifies that this container will remove itself upon being stopped. The *-dit* flag is to tell the container to start the container in the background while still allowing you to be able to attach to it. Using *--network* tells the container that it wants to connect to the macvlan network that you've created. Inspect the container with *$ docker macvlan-alpine-exercise*. There will be a lot of information here but we're specifically looking for the section about networks. It should look like:

"Networks": {

"test-macvlan-network": {

"IPAMConfig": null,

"Links": null,

"Aliases": [

"bec64291cd4c"

],

"NetworkID":" XXXXXXX",

"EndpointID": "XXXXXX",

"IPAddress": "172.16.86.1",

"IPPrefixLen": 24,

IPv6Gateway": "",

"GlobalIPv6Address": "",

"GlobalIPv6PrefixLen": 0,

"MacAddress": "02:42:ac:10:56:02",

"DriverOpts": null

}

}

Notice the second to last one, the MacAddress. This is the MAC address that has been assigned to the container for purposes of receiving traffic.

Use the command *$ docker exec test-macvlan-network ip addr show eth0* to see how the container perceives the network it is on. Another useful command for seeing how the container perceives the network is to use *$ docker exec test-macvlan-network ip route*.

You've now set up an Alpine container on a bridged macvlan network. Use *$ docker container stop macvlan-alpine-exercise* and *$docker network rm test-macvlan-network* to stop the container and remove the network. The container will remove itself since it was created with the *--rm* flag. Let's set up an 802.1q trunk bridge macvlan network now.

The 802.1q trunk bridge network uses a subinterface of eth0 to move your traffic before it is routed to the proper container via the MAC address. To begin, we'll create a new network:

*$ docker network create -d macvlan *

*--subnet=IP address of subnet/24 *

*--gateway=IP address of gateway *

*-o parent=eth0.10 *

test-8021q-network

Again, we use *$ docker network ls* and *$ docker network inspect test-8021q-network* in order to double check that everything was created properly. Always double check that your networks were created properly before working on them. Errors that may occur are the network failing to start, being started but not as a macvlan network, the network failing to set eth0.10 as its parent or failing to have a seperate IP address. Use *$ docker exec test-8021q-network ip addr show eth0.10* to check on the IP address. If everything checks out then the next step is launching the Alpine container with:

*$ docker run --rm -dit *

*--network test-8021q-network *

*--name 8021q-alpine-exercise *

*alpine:latest *

ash

By using the command *$ docker container inspect 8021q-alpine-exercise* you will get back the same report that you saw above. Again, you can find the

MAC address being used by the container as the second to last piece of information under the networks section. Use *$docker exec 8021q-alpine-exercise ip addr show eth0* and *$ docker exec 8021-q-alpine-exercise ip route* to see how the container views the network.

There you have it. You have now set up and attached a container to both types of macvlan networks. These are best used with legacy applications to trick them into thinking they are on a physical network. When you are done playing with your 802.1q trunk bridge macvlan network, remove the container and network by using *$ docker container stop 8021q-alpine exercise* and *$ docker network rm test-8021q-network.*

Exercise: Using None to Disable A Container From Networking Actions

There are many reasons that you might want to disable networking on a container. Regardless of what your reason is, you will do this through the same easy process. Once again we'll be using Alpine to practice. In previous exercises we started by first creating a network for the containers to then attach to. Since we're not actually looking to have our container network, we don't need to start a network. Instead, we begin by starting the container with:

```
$ docker run --rm -dit \
--network none \
--name none-alpine\
alpine:latest \
ash
```

Normally, the network we've created has a name and we use that with the *--network* flag. But since we want none, we use *none*. What this does is create a loopback device rather than a network. Let's check the status of the container's network stack using *$ docker exec none-alpine ip link show*. This should return these sections. The first should be a loopback, the second a NOARP and the third another NOARP. Try running *$ docker exec none-alpine ip route*. This should come back empty. This is because there is no routing table for the container. It isn't on the network. Stop the container with *$ docker container rm none-alpine*.

By simply setting the network as *none*, you remove all networking options from the container. It is important to remember that doing this actually takes the addition of the *--network none* flag. If you do not specify to Docker that you want this container running on *none* then Docker will automatically connect the container to the default bridge network when it is created.

Networking Containers

When networking with containers, each container will make it clear what kind of network it is using. Each container has a network interface that comes with an IP address, gateway, DNS services and routing table. Many will often have even more information than this. Not all, as containers created with none will lack all of this.

When you create a container, the default setting prevents it from telling the outside world about its ports. We need to use the *-p* or *--publish* flag in order to make a port available to the world outside of the container. This flag creates a rule in the firewall which allows us to map a port on the container to a port on the host. There are a couple ways this can be done.

-p 8080:80 has been used several times throughout the book. This simple command is used to map port 80 in the container to port 8080 on the host.

-p 192.168.1.100:8080:80 is used to map port 80 in the container onto the host's port 8080 but only for connections to the listed IP address.

-p 8080:80/udp is used to map the container's UDP port 80 to the host's port (8080).

-p 8080:80/tecp -p 8080:80/udp is about as complicated as publishing gets. This maps the container's TCP port 80 to the TCP port 8080 on the

host. It also maps the container's UDP port 80 the the specified UDP port of the host.

Containers are assigned IP addresses (unless otherwise told to) for every network they connect to. There is a pool of IP addresses assigned to each network. Docker pulls an IP address from this pool and then assigns it to the container. This lets Docker act like a DHCP server for each and every container. Each network will also have its own subnet and gateway address. A container can only be connected to one network when it is built; however, you can connect it to more networks after it is running. When connecting the container, with the *$ docker network connect* command, you can add the flag *--ip* or *--ip6* to set the IP address of the container on the new network.

Containers naturally take on the DNS settings of the Docker daemon but these can be changed for each container. The commands *--dns*, *--dns-search*, *--dns-opt* and *--hostname* are used to control this. *--hostname* allows you to set your own hostname for the container. The default is the container's ID. *--dns-opt* is used to set the key value for a DNS option. *--dns-search* is used to set a DNS search domain and *--dns* is used to specify an IP address for the DNS server. If you need to specify multiple DNS servers then simply use multiple *--dns* flags.

Chapter Summary

- Docker offers many options for networking and it is through the networking of containers that Docker proves to be such a powerful tool.

- The kinds of networks that Docker uses are bridge networks, overlay networks, host networks, macvlan networks or none.

- While Docker can be used on Linux, Windows or OS X, only Linux can use host networks or macvlan networks.

- The default network assigned to a newly created container is a bridge network.

- Docker EE includes session stickiness and HTTP routing mesh, options which users of the free Docker software will not have access to.

- Docker's bridge networks exist on the Link Layer and allow containers to communicate with each other so long as they use the same bridge.

- Docker has a default bridge network, or you can create a user-defined bridge network in order to gain much greater control over the network.

- There is no need to create a network if you plan on using the default bridge network. Also, since bridge networks are Docker's default, using the *$ docker network create* command will default to creating a bridge network. You can use *--driver bridge* to specify this to Docker but it isn't necessary.

- A container can only be added to a single network when it is created. When it is running it can be added to other networks. You can use this to connect a container to multiple bridges, which you may want to do to allow a container to act as a gateway between two different bridge networks.

- The host network driver is used to allow containers to work off of the host's network stack.

- A container using the host network functions as both isolated and not isolated. It uses the host's network stack but all of its files act within the container itself.

- Using the host network can help to improve performance and is recommended when using containers that use lots of ports.

- Launch a container with the *-network host* tag to set it on the host.

- An overlay network is a distributed network that functions on more than one Docker host. These hosts can be separate computers, virtual machines or cloud-based systems. Regardless of the hosts in question, you need at least two for an overlay network.

- Creating or joining a swarm will add two new networks to the Docker host. Ingress is an overlay network that controls swarm services and data and docker_gwbridge is a network which is used to connect the different Docker daemons to each other.

- A macvlan network is best used with legacy applications that monitor traffic on a network or those that need to be connected into a physical network. The macvlan network assigns a MAC address to each container and tricks the applications into thinking they are part of a physical networking setup.

- Macvlan networks can easily damage your network through IP address exhaustion or VLAN speed and they require networking gear that can handle promiscuous mode. Because of these issues, if your applications can use bridge networks or overlay networks then it is always better to use one of those.

- Macvlan networks have two modes: bridge or 802.1q trunk bridge. The 802.1q trunk bridge

147

mode is used to gain more control over the routing and filtering of traffic by routing traffic through a subinterface.

- The none driver is used to disable networking in a container. Simply launch your container with the *--network none* tag to remove networking from the container. If you launch the container without specifying then it will automatically connect to the default bridge network.

- Networking containers each have an IP address, gateway, DNS services and a routing table. Containers made with the none driver do not.

- Each network that Docker creates has a pool of IP addresses which it pulls from to assign an IP address to a container upon joining the network.

Final Words

If you've made it this far and worked on the exercises throughout the book then you are now well on your way to becoming a skilled Docker user. There is still plenty of room to grow. This was only the beginning of your journey towards expertise. With just the skills that you've learned already, you are more than capable of using Docker with your applications.

You may be using Docker for your DevOps workflow, in which case you should absolutely continue seeking out knowledge on Docker. There are many DevOps tools that we haven't been able to cover so far. With the knowledge you've just gained, you should have what you need to decide if Docker is right for your needs.

You now know what people mean when they talk about containers, images and Dockerfiles. These are the basic building blocks of containerizing applications. You even know how to containerize your own applications in order to run them within self-contained environments and make it easy to share your applications with friends and co-workers or even the world at large through Docker Hub. Many applications have already been turned into images on Docker Hub and you know how to find and use these to quickly get up and running on any system you use Docker on.

Finally, you've learned all about networking with Docker. While troubleshooting complicated networking problems was beyond the scope of this book, you've learned about and created your own bridge, overlay, host and macvlan networks. Each of these comes with its own challenges and their own purposes but you have everything you need to create and oversee any of your networking needs. It is through the networking of containers that Docker really shines.

If you are looking to continue learning about Docker then some topics of interest may be how to manage application data, how to run your applications during production or how to confirm Docker's daemon for IPv6 and the networking challenges that IPv6 brings with it. We've also only barely begun to touch on the challenges of using legacy content with Docker, a topic which could easily fill a book on its own.

Whatever direction you decide to study next, the grounding you have received from this volume will prove invaluable. I hope that you have found this book useful in understanding Docker and that you feel you have a much better understanding of how Docker works compared to when you started. Have fun running those containers!